PRENTICE HALL

Algebra 2

With Trigonometry

Practice Workbook

Prentice
Hall

Glenview, Illinois
Needham, Massachusetts
Upper Saddle River, New Jersey

ISBN 0-13-053358-0

3 4 5 6 7 8 9 10   04 03 02

Contents

Contents

Algebra One Review

The problems that follow may be used to evaluate your students' retention of algebraic concepts. When administered at the beginning of the academic year, the results can provide diagnostic information that will highlight areas of strengths and weaknesses in each student's algebra background. They also may be given to students to be used during the summer as a refresher for first-year algebra concepts.

Each group of 50 problems covers similar topics. Each successive set, however, increases in level of difficulty, with set C containing the most challenging exercises.

ALGEBRA ONE REVIEW

Set A

NAME _____

DATE _____

Directions: Show your work in the space provided and write your answer in the appropriate blank.

1. Evaluate $(x - 4) + 6$ for $x = 10$. 1. _____

2. Add: $-11.5 + 1.6 + (-5.2) + 0.7$ 2. _____

3. Multiply: $(-6)(7)$ 3. _____

4. Divide: $-\dfrac{1}{3} \div \dfrac{1}{15}$ 4. _____

5. What percent of 75 is 5? 5. _____

6. Solve for x: $5x - 12 = 48$ 6. _____

7. Solve for y: $y - 6 < 10$ 7. _____

8. Simplify: $a^3 \cdot a^2$ 8. _____

9. Multiply: $(-2x)(5x^2)$ 9. _____

10. Divide: $\dfrac{-10x^5}{2x^2}$ 10. _____

11. Add: $(3m^2 - 9) + (5m^3 - 2m^2 + 1)$ 11. _____

12. Multiply: $(2B - 1)(2B + 3)$ 12. _____

13. Factor: $m^5 - m^3$ 13. _____

14. Graph this equation on graph paper: $x + y = 4$ 14. _____ (Graph) _____

15. Find the slope and the y-intercept: $2y = -6x + 4$ 15. _____

16. Write the equation of the line containing the point (2, 5) and parallel to the x-axis. 16. _____

17. Is (4, 2) a solution to this system of equations? 17. _____
    $$x + y = 6$$
    $$2x - y = 6$$

18. Solve this system of equations: $y = x - 10$ 18. _____
    $$5y + 10x = 10$$

19. The difference of two numbers is 10. Two times the larger number is 20 more than the smaller. What are the two numbers? 19. _____

If $A = \{-10, -5, 0, 5, 10\}$ and $B = \{0, 1, 2, 3, 4, 5, 6, 7, 8, 9, 10\}$,

20. Find $A \cap B$ 20. _____

21. Find $A \cup B$ 21. _____

22. Solve and graph on a number line: $|x| < 6$ 22. _____

23. Multiply and simplify: 23. _____

$$\frac{8}{-3x + 6} \cdot \frac{3}{16x - 64}$$

24. Divide and simplify: 24. _____

$$\frac{x^2 - 9}{x^2 + 8x + 15} \div \frac{2x + 10}{x^2 + 4x + 5}$$

25. Subtract and simplify: 25. _____

$$\frac{2x^2}{2x + 5} - \frac{7x + 30}{2x + 5}$$

26. Solve: $\dfrac{x + 1}{x - 2} = \dfrac{3}{2}$ 26. _____

Simplify:

27. $\sqrt{25}$ 27. _____

28. $-\sqrt{100}$ 28. _____

29. $\sqrt{c^4 d^4}$ 29. _____

30. $\sqrt{20}$ 30. _____

31. $\sqrt{2a} \cdot \sqrt{2a}$ 31. _____

32. $\sqrt{3xy} \cdot \sqrt{4x^3 y}$ 32. _____

33. Rationalize the denominator: $\sqrt{\dfrac{1}{5}}$ 33. _____

34. Add: $5\sqrt{a} - 6\sqrt{a}$ 34. _____

35. In a right triangle with $a = 5$ and $b = 12$, find the length of   35. _____
hypotenuse c.

36. Find the indicated output for the function   36. _____
$f(x) = 3x^2 - 5x + 2$ when $x = -1$.

37. Graph $h(x) = x^2$ on graph paper.   37. _____ (Graph)

Solve. Leave answers in simplest radical form:

38. $2x^2 = 20$ 38. _____

39. $x^2 + 9 = 6x$ 39. _____

40. $p = \sqrt{2p + 8}$ 40. _____

41. Simplify. $\dfrac{x + 1}{x^2 - 1}$ 41. _____

42. In $\triangle xyz$ find sin x, cos x, and tan x.   42. _____

43. Use a table or a calculator to determine the degree   43. _____
measure of angle x to the nearest degree.

44. What is the measure of angle z to the nearest degree?   44. _____

45. What is the probability of drawing a king from a   45. _____
well-shuffled deck of 52 cards?

46. A bag contains 8 black marbles, 5 white marbles, and 1 red   46. _____
marble. If a marble is chosen at random, what is the
probability (in fractional form) that it will be red?

47. When spinning a spinner numbered 1 to 5, what is the   47. _____
probability of spinning a multiple of 2?

Justin earned the following math test grades: 73, 80, 75, 85, 85,
95, 97, 90.

48. Find the mean for this data.   48. _____

49. Find the median for this data.   49. _____

50. Find the mode for this data.   50. _____

ALGEBRA ONE REVIEW
Set B

NAME _____

DATE _____

Directions: Show your work in the space provided and write your answer in the appropriate blank.

1. Evaluate $(y - 2)^2 + (y + 5)^2$ for $y = -3$.

    1. _____

2. Add: $-\dfrac{1}{6} - 5 + \dfrac{2}{5} - \dfrac{1}{15}$

    2. _____

3. Multiply: $(-5.3)(2.1)$

    3. _____

4. Divide: $-\dfrac{2}{9} \div \dfrac{2}{3}$

    4. _____

5. 150 is what percent of 750?

    5. _____

6. Solve for x: $0.4x - 1.6 = 2.4x$

    6. _____

7. Solve for y: $8y - 3 > 2y + 15$

    7. _____

8. Simplify: $\dfrac{5m^7}{m^3}$

    8. _____

9. Multiply: $(-2x)(3x^2)$

    9. _____

10. Divide: $\dfrac{-27x^2y^3}{3xy}$

    10. _____

11. Subtract: $(-5a^2 - 2a) - (a^2 - 7a + 2)$

    11. _____

12. Multiply: $(a - 3)^2$

    12. _____

13. Factor: $49x^2 - 64$

    13. _____

14. Graph this equation on graph paper: $x = -3$

    14. _____ (Graph)

15. Find the slope and the y-intercept of this line: $5x - 10y = 250$

    15. _____

16. Write the equation for the line that contains the origin and $(-2, 4)$.

    16. _____

17. Is $(1, 2)$ a solution to this system of equations?
    $$3y = -6$$
    $$y = -2x + 1$$

    17. _____

18. Solve this system of equations: $2x - 3y = 10$
    $$-3x + y = 20$$

    18. _____

19. Lori is three times as old as Michelle. In five years Michelle's age will be one half of Lori's age. How old are Lori and Michelle now?

    19. _____

If A = the multiples of 4 and B = the multiples of 3,

20. Find $A \cap B$ **20.** _____

21. Find $A \cup \emptyset$ **21.** _____

22. Solve and graph on a number line: $|x - 2| \leq 3$ **22.** _____

23. Multiply and simplify: **23.** _____

$$\frac{x^3 - 25x}{x - 5} \cdot \frac{x + 10}{8x^2}$$

24. Divide and simplify: **24.** _____

$$\frac{y^2 - 49}{y^2 - 25} \div \frac{y^2 + 2y - 35}{5y + 25}$$

25. Subtract and simplify: **25.** _____

$$\frac{x - 4}{x} - \frac{x}{x + 3}$$

26. Solve: $\dfrac{6x}{x + 2} = \dfrac{3}{2}$ **26.** _____

27. Yolanda and Andrew are partners in a store. Yolanda   **27.** _____
invests $36,000 and Andrew invests $30,000. They agree to
share the profits in the ratio of the amount invested. The
profits for the first year were $11,000. How much should each
receive?

28. Determine replacements for x that will make the expression   **28.** _____
a real number:

$$\sqrt{x - 3}$$

29. Simplify: $\sqrt{a^2 b^2}$ **29.** _____

30. Simplify: $\sqrt{64a^2}$ **30.** _____

31. Multiply: $\sqrt{3x} \cdot \sqrt{4y}$ **31.** _____

32. Factor and simplify: $\sqrt{48x^3 y^4}$ **32.** _____

33. Multiply and simplify: $\sqrt{3ab^2 c^3 d^4} \cdot \sqrt{30a^4 b^3 c^2 d}$ **33.** _____

34. Rationalize and simplify: $\dfrac{\sqrt{5}}{\sqrt{10}}$ **34.** _____

35. Add: $\sqrt{225y^3} + \sqrt{169y^3}$ **35.** _____

36. In a right triangle where c is the hypotenuse and $a = 1$ and   **36.** _____
$c = \sqrt{5}$, find the length of b.

37. Find the indicated output $f(-1)$ if $f(x) = x^4 - 7x^3 + 2$.

37. _____

38. Graph on graph paper: $g(x) = 2x^2 - 1$

38. _____(Graph)_____

39. When you swim underwater, the pressure in your ears varies directly as the depth at which you swim. At 20 feet the pressure is 8.6 pounds per square inch (psi). Find the pressure at 60 feet.

39. _____

40. Solve: $x^2 + 16 = 8x$

40. _____

41. Solve: $3\sqrt{x^2 - 9} = x + 3$

41. _____

42. The width of a rectangle is one-fourth of its length. The area is 64 m². Find the length and the width.

42. _____

43. In right $\triangle ABC$ $\angle B = 60^\circ$. Find sin A, cos A, and tan A rounded to four decimal places.

43. _____

44. What is the probability of drawing a card that is not a face card from a well-shuffled deck of 52 cards?

44. _____

45. When spinning a spinner numbered 1 to 8, what is the probability of spinning an even number or a multiple of 5?

45. _____

46. A bag contains 6 blue marbles, 2 yellow marbles, and 1 red marble. If a marble is chosen at random, what is the probability (in fractional form) that it will be blue or red?

46. _____

During ten weeks of babysitting Jessica earned the following dollar amounts: 30, 33, 35, 50, 50, 60, 65, 90, 50, 35

47. Find the mean for this data to the nearest dollar.

47. _____

48. Find the median for this data.

48. _____

49. Find the mode(s) for this data.

49. _____

50. Construct a histogram for this data.

50. _____

ALGEBRA ONE REVIEW

Set C

NAME _____

DATE _____

Directions: Show your work in the space provided and write your answer in the appropriate blank.

1. Evaluate $(x - y)^2 + 2(x + y)$ for $x = 9$ and $y = -2$.

    1. _____

2. Simplify: $23a^2 - 17b - 3a^2 - b + 5$

    2. _____

3. Simplify: $\left(-\dfrac{2}{3}\right)\left(\dfrac{1}{5}\right) - \left(\dfrac{7}{15} \div \dfrac{28}{3}\right)$

    3. _____

4. What is 25% of 25% of 150 to the nearest tenth?

    4. _____

5. Solve: $-\dfrac{2}{5}x + 2 = \dfrac{3}{10}x + \dfrac{x}{4}$

    5. _____

6. Two fifths of the automobiles entering the city every morning will be parked in city parking lots. These cars fill 5282 parking spaces. How many cars enter the city each morning?

    6. _____

7. The new City Council representative won by a ratio of 6 to 5, with 2343 total votes cast. How many votes did she get?

    7. _____

8. Solve: $23 - 7x - 3x \geq -7$

    8. _____

9. A rectangular wading pool will be 4.5 m wide. What length will make the area at least 54 m²?

    9. _____

10. Simplify: $\dfrac{(2x^5 y^3)^2}{(6x)^3}$

    10. _____

11. Multiply: $-4x^2 y^3 z^5 (2xy^2 - z)$

    11. _____

12. Divide: $-50a^2 bc \div 2.5a^3 c^{-1}$

    12. _____

13. Add: $(-7a^3 - 2a^2 + 5) + (-5a^4 + 3a^3 - 6a^2 - 1)$

    13. _____

14. Multiply: $(2m - 6)^3$

    14. _____

15. Factor: $x^3 - 50x^2 + 625x$

    15. _____

16. Factor: $30x^4 + 21x^3 - 36x^2$

    16. _____

17. Find the slope and the *y*-intercept of this line: $3y - 5x - 2 = 0$

    17. _____

18. Write an equation in slope-intercept form for the line that has *x*-intercept 5 and *y*-intercept -2.

    18. _____

19. Solve this system of equations:
    $$2x = 3y + 12$$
    $$2x + 5y = 8$$

    19. _____

20. For the school musical, 475 tickets were sold. Student tickets sold for $1.50 and adult tickets sold for $2.75. If the total amount received was $977.50, how many tickets of each kind were sold?

20. _____

21. If A = multiples of 3, B = factors of 12, $C = \varnothing$, find $(A \cap B) \cup C$?

21. _____

22. Solve and graph on a number line: $4|z + 3| \geq 8$

22. _____

23. Multiply and simplify: $\dfrac{3 - x}{x^4 - 81} \cdot \dfrac{3x^3 - 27x}{x^2 - 4x + 3}$

23. _____

24. Divide and simplify: $\dfrac{4a^2 + 12a + 9}{5a^4} \div \dfrac{2a^2 + 5a + 3}{-20a^3}$

24. _____

25. Subtract and simplify: $\dfrac{n + 4}{n - 1} - \dfrac{n}{n + 1}$

25. _____

26. Solve: $\dfrac{6}{x - 4} = \dfrac{5}{x - 3}$

26. _____

27. Determine replacements for x that will make the expression a real number:
$$\sqrt{-2x + 4}$$

27. _____

28. Simplify: $\sqrt{(x + 3)^2}$

28. _____

29. Multiply: $\sqrt{x - 3} \cdot \sqrt{x + 3}$

29. _____

30. Factor and simplify: $\sqrt{25x - 175}$

30. _____

31. Rationalize the denominator and simplify: $\sqrt{\dfrac{x^2}{12}}$

31. _____

32. Subtract: $2x\sqrt{x^3y^2} - y\sqrt{x^2y^2} - 4\sqrt{x^3}$

32. _____

33. Find the indicated output for the function
$$f(x) = 2x^3 - 3x^2 - 5x - 1 \text{ for } f\left(-\dfrac{1}{3}\right).$$

33. _____

34. Graph the equation $g(x) = -\dfrac{1}{2}x^2$ on graph paper.

34. _____ (Graph)

35. A 26-foot ladder is leaning against a building. The bottom of the ladder is 10 ft. from the building. How high is the top of the ladder?

35. _____

36. The amount that a family gives to charity varies directly as its income. Last year, the family earned $30,720 and gave $6,144 to charity. How much did they earn this year if they will give $7,056 to charity?

36. _____

37. Solve: $8x^2 + 10x - 3 = 0$

37. _____

38. Solve: $1 + \dfrac{4}{x} = \dfrac{5}{x^2}$

38. _____

39. Solve: $\sqrt{x^2 - 25} = x + 5$ 39. _____

40. One leg of a right triangle is 7 cm longer than the other. The hypotenuse is 17 cm long. Find the lengths of the legs.   40. _____

41. An angle of a triangle is twice as large as another angle. The third angle is six times as large as the smallest angle. What are the measures of all three angles?   41. _____

Refer to the diagram of $\triangle DEF$ for Exercises 42–45.

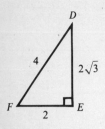

42. Express cos F as a ratio in lowest terms.   42. _____

43. Find sin F to four decimal places.   43. _____

44. What is the measure of $\angle F$ in degrees?   44. _____

45. Find the measure of $\angle D$.   45. _____

46. The angle of elevation of a jetliner is 15°. The distance to the jetliner is 20 km. How high is the jetliner to the nearest tenth of a km?   46. _____

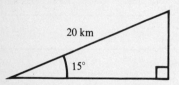

47. The top of a lighthouse is 180 m above water level. The angle of depression from the top of the lighthouse to a motorboat is 37°. How far from the base of the lighthouse is the motorboat to the nearest tenth of a meter?   47. _____

A bag contains 3 orange marbles, 2 purple marbles, and 28 green marbles. If a marble is chosen at random,

48. What is the probability (as a ratio in lowest terms) that it will be either orange or purple?   48. _____

49. What is the probability that an orange, purple, or green marble will be chosen?   49. _____

50. What is the probability that a grey marble will be chosen?   50. _____

Skills Practice Worksheets

The following 51 blackline masters are worksheets for skills practice. Each provides additional exercises for one to four consecutive lessons in the text. The exercises have been modeled after the Examples, Try This, and A-level Exercises found in the student text.

You will find these worksheets helpful for students needing extra practice on fundamental concepts. These worksheets can also be incorporated within the context of a chapter or cumulative review.

SKILLS PRACTICE 17

For use with Lessons 6-7 through 6-9

NAME _____

DATE _____

6-7   Solve.

1. The tram at Valley View Ski Resort can transport 5000 people in 6 hours. Using the chairlift and tram, 5000 people can be brought to the top in 2 hours. If the tram breaks, how long will it take the chairlift to bring 5000 to the mountaintop?

                         _____

2. A plane can travel 350 km/h in still air. With the wind it flew 1000 km. In the same amount of time it could travel 750 km against the wind. Find the speed of the wind.

                         _____

6-8   Solve each formula for the given letter.

3. $\dfrac{k_1}{k_2} = \dfrac{x_1}{x_2}$; k_2 _____

4. $\dfrac{1}{r_1} + \dfrac{1}{r_2} = \dfrac{1}{R}$; r_1 _____

5. $\dfrac{1}{c_1} + \dfrac{1}{c_2} = \dfrac{1}{C}$; c_2 _____

6. $a = \dfrac{v_1 + v_2}{t_1 + t_2}$; t_2 _____

7. $m^2 = \dfrac{m_0^2 c^2}{c^2 + v^2}$; m_0^2 _____

8. $t^2 = \dfrac{t_0^2 c^2}{c^2 + v^2}$; v^2 _____

6-8   Solve.

9. One resistor has a resistance of 18 ohms. What size resistor should be connected with it, in parallel, to obtain a resistance of 12 ohms?

                         _____

6-9   Find the constant of variation and an equation of variation where (a) y varies directly as x and (b) y varies inversely as x.

10. $y = 8$ when $x = 4$;   **a.** _____   **b.** _____

11. $y = 11$ when $x = 5$;   **a.** _____   **b.** _____

12. $y = 4$ when $x = 6$;   **a.** _____   **b.** _____

13. $y = 9$ when $x = \dfrac{1}{3}$;   **a.** _____   **b.** _____

6-9   Solve.

14. The power (P), in watts, in a circuit varies directly as the current (I), in amperes. When the current is 2 amperes, the power used is 240 watts. What is the current when 600 watts is used?

                         _____

15. The acceleration (a) of an object, produced by a fixed force, varies inversely as the object's mass (m). A fixed force produces an acceleration of 30 m/s² for an object of 5 kg. For an object of 25 kg, what is the resulting acceleration?

                         _____

7-1   Find the following. Assume that variables represent any real number.

1. $-\sqrt{\dfrac{36}{49}}$ _____

2. $\sqrt{169}$ _____

3. $\sqrt{0.09}$ _____

4. $\sqrt[3]{-1}$ _____

5. $\sqrt{0.0001}$ _____

6. $\sqrt{361}$ _____

7. $\sqrt{(a-b)^2}$ _____

8. $\sqrt{(ab)^2}$ _____

9. $\sqrt[3]{0.008x^3}$ _____

10. $-\sqrt[3]{-64x^3}$ _____

11. $\sqrt[3]{-27x^3y^6}$ _____

12. $\sqrt[4]{81}$ _____

13. $\sqrt[5]{-32x^5}$ _____

14. $\sqrt[7]{x^7}$ _____

15. $\sqrt[6]{(3x-4)^6}$ _____

7-2   Multiply and simplify by factoring, if possible. Assume expressions under radical signs represent nonnegative numbers.

16. $\sqrt{7x}\sqrt{2y}$ _____

17. $\sqrt[3]{4x}\sqrt[3]{9x}$ _____

18. $\sqrt{\dfrac{5}{a}}\sqrt{\dfrac{b}{6}}$ _____

19. $\sqrt{98}$ _____

20. $\sqrt{200a^6}$ _____

21. $\sqrt[3]{48x^3y^6}$ _____

22. $\sqrt{21}\sqrt{3}$ _____

23. $\sqrt{18c}\sqrt{2c}$ _____

24. $\sqrt{8a^3b}\sqrt{12ab^3}$ _____

25. $\sqrt{6x^3}\sqrt{18x^4}$ _____

26. $\sqrt[3]{25x^2}\sqrt[3]{10x^2}$ _____

27. $\sqrt[3]{16y^4}\sqrt[3]{8y^5}$ _____

28. $\sqrt[3]{(a+b)^5}$ _____

29. $\sqrt[3]{81x^{10}y^7}$ _____

30. $\sqrt[4]{(a+b)^5}$ _____

31. $\sqrt[4]{81x^{10}y^7}$ _____

7-3   Simplify by finding roots of the numerator and denominator.

32. $\sqrt{\dfrac{64}{49}}$ _____

33. $\sqrt[3]{\dfrac{125}{64}}$ _____

34. $\sqrt{\dfrac{81}{a^4}}$ _____

35. $\sqrt[3]{\dfrac{8a^3}{27b^6}}$ _____

7-3   Divide. Then simplify by finding roots, if possible.

36. $\dfrac{\sqrt{125x^3}}{\sqrt{5x}}$ _____

37. $\dfrac{\sqrt{243}}{\sqrt{3}}$ _____

38. $\dfrac{\sqrt[3]{24a^5}}{\sqrt[3]{3a^2}}$ _____

39. $\dfrac{\sqrt{108ab^3}}{3\sqrt{3ab}}$ _____

40. $\dfrac{\sqrt[3]{48c^3d^8}}{2\sqrt[3]{6d^2}}$ _____

41. $\dfrac{\sqrt{x^2-y^2}}{\sqrt{x-y}}$ _____

7-3   Add or subtract. Simplify by collecting like radical terms, if possible.

42. $4\sqrt{5}+7\sqrt{5}-8\sqrt{5}$ _____

43. $8\sqrt{6}-2\sqrt{3}+\sqrt{6}+4\sqrt{3}$ _____

44. $2\sqrt{27}+4\sqrt{3}-3\sqrt{12}$ _____

45. $6\sqrt[3]{16}-2\sqrt[3]{54}$ _____

46. $\sqrt[3]{27x}+\sqrt[3]{8x^4}$ _____

47. $\sqrt[3]{16a^5}-\sqrt[3]{2a^2}+\sqrt[3]{54a^2}$ _____

48. $\sqrt{x^3+x^2}+\sqrt{4x+4}$ _____

49. $\sqrt{x^4-x^2}-\sqrt{x^2-1}$ _____

Assume all variables represent nonnegative real numbers.

7-4 Multiply.

1. $\sqrt{5}(4 - 2\sqrt{5})$ _____

2. $\sqrt{2}(3\sqrt{6} + 2\sqrt{2})$ _____

3. $\sqrt{3}(\sqrt{12} + 2\sqrt{27})$ _____

4. $(2\sqrt{7} + \sqrt{3})(2\sqrt{7} - \sqrt{3})$ _____

5. $\sqrt[3]{5}(\sqrt[3]{25} - \sqrt[3]{75})$ _____

6. $\sqrt[3]{y}(\sqrt[3]{9y^2} + \sqrt[3]{8y^2})$ _____

7-4 Rationalize the denominator.

7. $\sqrt{\dfrac{7}{11}}$ _____

8. $\sqrt[3]{\dfrac{11}{25}}$ _____

9. $\dfrac{\sqrt{7}}{4\sqrt{a}}$ _____

10. $\dfrac{\sqrt[3]{4a}}{\sqrt[3]{3b}}$ _____

11. $\dfrac{2}{x - \sqrt{y}}$ _____

12. $\dfrac{5\sqrt{3} - 2\sqrt{5}}{3\sqrt{5} - 2\sqrt{3}}$ _____

7-5 Write with rational exponents.

13. $\sqrt[3]{a^2b^2}$ _____

14. $\sqrt[7]{c^3}$ _____

15. $\sqrt[3]{a^4b^7}$ _____

7-5 Write with positive exponents.

16. $x^{-\frac{1}{3}}$ _____

17. $\left(\dfrac{1}{x}\right)^{-\frac{2}{3}}$ _____

18. $\dfrac{1}{a^{-\frac{3}{4}}}$ _____

7-5 Use the properties of exponents to simplify.

19. $6^{\frac{1}{3}}6^{\frac{3}{5}}$ _____

20. $(7^{\frac{1}{3}})^{\frac{3}{5}}$ _____

21. $\dfrac{11^{\frac{3}{7}}}{11^{\frac{5}{7}}}$ _____

22. $\dfrac{5^{\frac{7}{9}}}{5^{\frac{2}{9}}}$ _____

7-5 Write as a single radical expression.

23. $a^{\frac{1}{3}}b^{\frac{3}{5}}$ _____

24. $\dfrac{x^{\frac{5}{12}}y^{\frac{5}{6}}}{x^{\frac{1}{3}}y^{-\frac{1}{3}}}$ _____

7-6 Solve.

25. $\sqrt{3x - 2} = 2$ _____

26. $\sqrt{x + 1} - 4 = 1$ _____

27. $4\sqrt{y} = 12$ _____

28. $\sqrt[3]{x - 4} = 2$ _____

29. $6 = \dfrac{1}{\sqrt{x}}$ _____

30. $\sqrt{y + 7} = -6$ _____

31. $3\sqrt{a - 2} = \sqrt{8a + 1}$ _____

32. $2\sqrt{x + 3} = \sqrt{6x - 4}$ _____

SKILLS PRACTICE 20

For use with Lessons 7-7 through 7-10

NAME _____

DATE _____

7-7 Express these numbers in terms of i.

1. $\sqrt{-3}$ _____   **2.** $\sqrt{-49}$ _____   **3.** $\sqrt{-18}$ _____

4. $-\sqrt{-27}$ _____   **5.** $\sqrt{-50}$ _____   **6.** $-\sqrt{-32}$ _____

7-7 Multiply.

7. $17i \cdot 3$ _____   **8.** $-8i(-4i)$ _____

9. $\sqrt{-2}(-5i)$ _____   **10.** $-\sqrt{-12}\sqrt{-3}$ _____

11. $\sqrt{-6}\sqrt{-3}$ _____   **12.** $-\sqrt{-9}(-\sqrt{-9})$ _____

7-7 Add or subtract.

13. $7i + 2i$ _____   **14.** $-8i + 12i$ _____

15. $-3i + (-4 + 6i)$ _____   **16.** $(2 - 5i) + (4 - i)$ _____

17. $6i - 2i$ _____   **18.** $-5i - (-3i)$ _____

19. $3i - (7 - 2i)$ _____   **20.** $(-4 - 3i) - (3 - 4i)$ _____

7-8 Find the absolute values.

21. $|1 + i|$ _____   **22.** $|1 - i|$ _____   **23.** $|3 - 4i|$ _____

7-9 Solve for x and y.

24. $3x - 4i = -6 + yi$ _____   **25.** $6 + 6yi = 2x - 3i$ _____

26. $4x - yi = 12 + 7i$ _____   **27.** $-2y + 5xi = 3 + 10i$ _____

7-9 Multiply or divide.

28. $4i \cdot 7i$ _____   **29.** $(8i)^2$ _____   **30.** $(-6i)^2$ _____

31. $(4 - 3i)(4 + 3i)$ _____   **32.** $(\sqrt{2} + i)(\sqrt{2} - i)$ _____

33. $\dfrac{1 + i}{i}$ _____   **34.** $\dfrac{4 + 5i}{-2 + 3i}$ _____

7-10 Find an equation having the specified numbers as solutions.

35. $i, -i$ _____   **36.** $2 + 2i, 2 - 2i$ _____

7-10 Solve.

37. $(2 - i)x = 2 + i$ _____   **38.** $(2 - 3i)x + 2i = -4 - 3i$ _____

39. $3ix + 4 = (1 + i)x - 2i$ _____   **40.** $(4 - 3i)x + 3i = (2 - i)x + 2 - i$ _____

8-1   Solve.

1. $x^2 - 8x + 7 = 0$ _____   2. $x^2 + 11x + 18 = 0$ _____

3. $8x^2 - 2x - 3 = 0$ _____   4. $4y^2 + 9x - 9 = 0$ _____

5. $9x^2 + 6x - 8 = 0$ _____   6. $(y + 4)(y - 1) = 24$ _____

7. $4b(3b + 6) = -9$ _____   8. $4x(x + 1) = (2x + 3)(x - 5)$ _____

9. $2x^2 + 5x = 12$ _____   10. $p(3p + 2) = 5$ _____   11. $3x^2 = 18$ _____

12. $-4t^2 + 3 = 0$ _____   13. $16x^2 + 25 = 0$ _____   14. $4x^2 + 12 = 0$ _____

15. $\dfrac{9}{16}x^2 - 1 = 0$ _____   16. $3x^2 = 10$ _____   17. $9x^2 + 25 = 0$ _____

18. $4x^2 + 20x = 0$ _____   19. $8x^2 - 5x = 0$ _____   20. $x^2 + 9x = 0$ _____

8-1   Solve by completing the square.

21. $x^2 + 4x = 1$ _____   22. $y^2 + 6y + 7 = 0$ _____   23. $x^2 + 7x + 1 = 0$ _____

8-2   Solve.

24. The width of a rectangular mural is 5 m less than the height. The area is 126 m². Find the height and the width. _____

25. The outside of a picture frame measures 13 cm by 18 cm. 176 cm² of picture shows inside the frame. Find the width of the frame. _____

26. The outside of a picture frame measures 15 cm by 20 cm. 176 cm² of picture shows inside the frame. Find the width of the frame. _____

8-3   Solve.

27. $x^2 + 6x + 2 = 0$ _____   28. $x^2 - 5x - 14 = 0$ _____

29. $t^2 + 4t = 21$ _____   30. $3p^2 + 2p - 5 = 0$ _____

31. $5x^2 = 13x - 6$ _____   32. $x^2 - 2x + 3 = 0$ _____

33. $m^2 + 11 = 6m$ _____   34. $x^2 + 7 = 0$ _____

35. $2x + x(x - 3) = 0$ _____   36. $4t^2 + 2t + 1 = 0$ _____

8-4   Determine the nature of the solutions of each equation.

1. $x^2 + 4x - 5 = 0$ _____

2. $y^2 - 10y + 25 = 0$ _____

3. $4x^2 + 4x + 1 = 0$ _____

4. $x^2 + 4x + 5 = 0$ _____

5. $9a^2 - 6a = 0$ _____

6. $3x^2 + 3x + 1 = 0$ _____

7. $x^2 - 8x + 16 = 0$ _____

8. $x^2 + 5 = 0$ _____

9. $x^2 - 5 = 0$ _____

10. $9y^2 - 12y + 4 = 0$ _____

11. $x^2 + 3x + 7 = 0$ _____

12. $5p^2 + 2p = 0$ _____

8-4   Find the sum and product of the solutions.

13. $x^2 + 5x + 6 = 0$ _____

14. $x^2 - x - 1 = 0$ _____

15. $10 - 2x^2 + 6x = 0$ _____

16. $3x^2 + 4x - 9 = 0$ _____

17. $p^2 = 36$ _____

18. $(3 + 2x)^2 = 5x$ _____

8-4   Find a quadratic equation for which the sum and product of the solutions are as given.

19. Sum $= -3$; product $= \dfrac{2}{3}$ _____

20. Sum $= \dfrac{3}{4}$; product $= -\dfrac{1}{2}$ _____

8-4   Find a quadratic equation whose solution or solutions are the following.

21. $1, 2$ _____

22. $-5, 1$ _____

23. $0, 6$ _____

8-4   Use the sum and product properties to write a quadratic equation whose solutions are the following.

24. $-2, -1$ _____

25. $3, 7$ _____

26. $3, -\dfrac{1}{2}$ _____

8-5   Solve.

27. $x^4 - 8x^2 + 16 = 0$ _____

28. $x^4 - 6x^2 + 5 = 0$ _____

29. $-12y^{-2} + y^{-1} + 1 = 0$ _____

30. $x - 13\sqrt{x} + 36 = 0$ _____

31. $t^{\frac{2}{3}} + 3t^{\frac{1}{3}} - 10 = 0$ _____

32. $r^{\frac{1}{2}} - 7r^{\frac{1}{4}} + 12 = 0$ _____

33. $s^{\frac{1}{3}} - s^{\frac{1}{6}} - 2 = 0$ _____

34. $\sqrt[3]{q^2} + 5\sqrt[3]{q} + 6 = 0$ _____

35. $x - 7\sqrt{x} + 6 = 0$ _____

36. $3x - 10\sqrt{x} + 3 = 0$ _____

37. $x^4 - 12x^2 + 36 = 0$ _____

38. $x^4 + 4x^2 - 5 = 0$ _____

39. $x^4 - 4x^2 + 1 = 0$ _____

40. $x^{-2} + x^{-1} - 12 = 0$ _____

8-6 ____ Solve for the indicated letter.

1. $V = hw^2$; w _____

2. $x = \frac{1}{2}at^2$; t _____

3. $\sqrt{\frac{F}{k}} = x$; F _____

4. $F = \frac{kq_1q_2}{r^2}$; r _____

5. $P = I^2R$; I _____

6. $P = \frac{V^2}{R}$; V _____

7. $h = 2v + 10t^2$; t _____

8. $x = \frac{1}{2}at^2 + vt$; t _____

9. $t^2 + 3g = \pi t$; t _____

8-6 ____ Solve. Use the formula $s = 0.8t^2 + v_0t$ (for objects falling to the moon).

10. a. If an object is dropped from an orbiting spacecraft that is 5000 m above the surface of the moon, how long does it take to reach the ground? _____

b. If the spacecraft's initial downward velocity is 100 m/s and the braking rockets fail to fire, how long does it take the spacecraft to reach the ground? _____

c. If the braking rockets fire, the equation of motion changes to $s = -\frac{1}{2}t^2 + 100t$. How far will the spacecraft fall in 100 seconds? _____

8-7 ____ Find an equation of variation where

11. y varies directly as the square of x, and $y = 80$ when $x = 4$. _____

12. y varies inversely as the square of x, and $y = 5$ when $x = 3$. _____

13. z varies jointly as x and y, and $z = 42$ when $x = 2$ and $y = 7$. _____

14. z varies directly as x and inversely as y, and $z = 1$ when $x = 4$ and $y = 4$. _____

15. w varies jointly as x and y and inversely as the square of z, and $w = 9$ when $x = 3$, $y = 6$, and $z = 2$.

_____

8-7 ____ Solve.

16. The force (F) due to gravity varies inversely as the square of the distance (r) between two objects. If the gravitational force between Peter and Rocío is 50 dynes when they are 2 cm apart, find the force of attraction when they are 10 cm apart. _____

9-1   Solve.

     1. Plot $(2, -4)$ and the point symmetric to it with respect to the x-axis, y-axis, and origin. List the coordinates of each point. _____

9-1   Test for symmetry with respect to the axes.

     2. $2y = x^2 + 5$ _____   **3.** $6y = 3x^2 - 4$ _____   **4.** $5x^4 + 2 = y^2$ _____

     5. $2x^2 - 3y^2 = 9$ _____   **6.** $2y^2 = x^3$ _____   **7.** $x^3 - 2y^3 = 7$ _____

9-1   Test for symmetry with respect to the origin.

     8. $2x^2 - 5y^2 = 4$ _____   **9.** $5x + 5y = 0$ _____   **10.** $7x = 7y$ _____

     11. $5x = \dfrac{7}{y}$ _____   **12.** $5x^2 + 2x = 6y$ _____   **13.** $y = |6x|$ _____

9-1   Determine whether each function is even, odd, or neither.

     14. $f(x) = -2x^3 + 5x$ _____   **15.** $f(x) = 2x + \dfrac{4}{x}$ _____

     16. $f(x) = 5x^4 - 2x^2$ _____   **17.** $f(x) = |7x|$ _____

     18. $f(x) = 3x - |2x|$ _____   **19.** $f(x) = 4x^2 + 6x$ _____

9-2   Sketch these graphs by translating the graph of $y = f(x)$.

     20. $y = f(x) + 1$ **21.** $y = f(x) - 2$

     22. $y = f(x) - 4$ **23.** $y = f(x) + \dfrac{1}{2}$

     24. $y = f(x + 1)$ **25.** $y = f(x - 2)$

$y = f(x)$

9-3   Sketch these graphs using $y = f(x)$.

     26. $y = 2f(x)$ **27.** $y = \dfrac{1}{2}f(x)$ **28.** $y = -2f(x)$

     29. $y = -\dfrac{1}{2}f(x)$ **30.** $y = 3f(x)$ **31.** $y = -\dfrac{1}{4}f(x)$

     32. $y = f(2x)$ **33.** $y = f\left(\dfrac{1}{2}x\right)$ **34.** $y = f(-2x)$

     35. $y = f\left(-\dfrac{1}{2}x\right)$ **36.** $y = f(4x)$ **37.** $y = f\left(-\dfrac{1}{4}x\right)$

SKILLS PRACTICE 25

For use with Lessons 9-4 through 9-5

NAME _____

DATE _____

9-4   Graph the function, find the vertex, and find the line of symmetry for each of the following.

1. $f(x) = 3x^2$ _____

2. $f(x) = -3x^2$ _____

3. $f(x) = \frac{1}{3}x^2$ _____

4. $f(x) = -\frac{1}{3}x^2$ _____

5. $f(x) = 3(x + 4)^2$ _____

6. $f(x) = (x + 4)^2$ _____

7. $f(x) = -3(x - 4)^2$ _____

8. $f(x) = 3(x - 4)^2$ _____

9. $f(x) = -\frac{1}{3}(x + 4)^2$ _____

10. $f(x) = \frac{1}{3}(x + 4)^2$ _____

11. $f(x) = -4(x - 7)^2$ _____

12. $f(x) = -5(x - 6)^2$ _____

9-5   Graph the function, find the vertex, find the line of symmetry, and find the minimum or maximum value for each of the following.

13. $f(x) = (x + 1)^2 + 1$ _____

14. $f(x) = -(x - 1)^2 - 1$ _____

15. $f(x) = -(x + 2)^2 - 2$ _____

16. $f(x) = (x - 2)^2 + 2$ _____

17. $f(x) = -4(x - 3)^2 + 5$ _____

18. $f(x) = 4(x + 4)^2 + 4$ _____

9-5   Without graphing, find the vertex, find the line of symmetry, and find the minimum or maximum value.

19. $f(x) = -2(x + 3)^2 + 4$ _____

20. $f(x) = -3(x - 4)^2 - 2$ _____

21. $f(x) = 4(x - 1)^2 - 3$ _____

22. $f(x) = 4(x + 1)^2 + 2$ _____

23. $f(x) = 2.5(x - \sqrt{3})^2 - \pi$ _____

24. $f(x) = 2\pi(x + 5.6)^2 + \sqrt{17}$ _____

Complete the chart.

	Function	What is the vertex?	What is the line of symmetry?	Is there a maximum?	Is there a minimum? What is it?
25.	$f(x) = 7(x - 5)^2 + 4$	$(5, 4)$			
26.	$f(x) = -9(x + 4)^2 - 6$				
27.	$f(x) = -3(x - 6)^2 + 13$				
28.	$f(x) = 10(x + 9)^2 - 21$		$x = -$		
29.	$f(x) = -5(x - 7)^2 - 14$	$(7, -14)$			
30.	$f(x) = -8(x + 11)^2 + 25$				

9-6 ___ For each function find standard form, the vertex, the line of symmetry, and the maximum or minimum value.

1. $f(x) = x^2 - 6x + 13$ _____

2. $f(x) = -x^2 - 4x - 6$ _____

3. $f(x) = -3x^2 + 6x - 1$ _____

4. $f(x) = 2x^2 + 16x + 29$ _____

9-6 ___ Solve.

5. A farmer is subdividing a portion of his farm for his livestock. He will make the area rectangular and will fix the perimeter at 100 m with fencing he already owns. What dimensions would yield the maximum area? What is the maximum area? _____

9-7 ___ Find the x-intercepts.

6. $f(x) = x^2 + 2x - 15$ _____ **7.** $f(x) = 9x^2 + 12x + 4$ _____

8. $f(x) = x^2 - 4x + 2$ _____ **9.** $f(x) = x^2 + 6x + 10$ _____

10. $f(x) = x^2 + 4x + 13$ _____ **11.** $f(x) = 4x^2 + 20x + 25$ _____

9-8 ___ Find the quadratic function that fits each set of data points.

12. $(1, 2), (3, 14), (-1, 14)$ _____ **13.** $(0, 5), (2, 15), (-2, 3)$ _____

14. $(1, 7), (-1, -7), (-2, -8)$ _____ **15.** $(1, 3), (2, 12), (-1, 9)$ _____

9-8 ___ Solve.

16. A new floral shop makes a gross profit of $600 in its first month, $400 in its third month, and $1000 in its fifth month. The owner plots the points (1, 600), (3, 400), and (5, 1000).
  a. Find a quadratic function that fits the data. _____
  b. Predict how much gross profit the shop will make in its seventh month. _____

10-1   Find the distance between the points.

1. $(-2, -5)$ and $(4, 3)$ _____

2. $(3, 7)$ and $(-1, 4)$ _____

3. $(1, 2)$ and $(-3, -2)$ _____

4. $(0, 1)$ and $(2, -3)$ _____

5. $(2b, -2)$ and $(b, -7)$ _____

6. $(0, 0)$ and (s, t) _____

10-1   Find the midpoint of the segments having the following endpoints.

7. $(-4, -7)$ and $(-6, -11)$ _____

8. $(-5, 6)$ and $(3, -2)$ _____

9. $(2, -5)$ and $(-5, -3)$ _____

10. $(3, 3)$ and $(7, 7)$ _____

10-2   Find an equation of a circle with the given center and radius.

11. $(0, 0)$; 5 _____

12. $(3, 5)$; $\sqrt{6}$ _____

10-2   Find the center and the radius of each circle. Then graph the circle.

13. $(x + 2)^2 + (y - 1)^2 = 9$ _____

14. $(x - 4)^2 + (y + 4)^2 = 1$ _____

15. $(x - 5)^2 + (y + 2)^2 = 16$ _____

16. $(x + 3)^2 + (y + 3)^2 = 18$ _____

17. $x^2 + y^2 = 5$ _____

18. $(x + 4)^2 + y^2 = \dfrac{1}{9}$ _____

10-2   Find the center and the radius of each circle.

19. $x^2 + y^2 - 4x - 4y + 4 = 0$ _____

20. $x^2 + y^2 + 2x - 6y + 1 = 0$ _____

10-3   For each ellipse find the center, the vertices, and the foci, and draw a graph.

21. $\dfrac{x^2}{36} + \dfrac{y^2}{9} = 1$ _____

22. $4x^2 + y^2 = 4$ _____

23. $9x^2 + 4y^2 = 36$ _____

24. $3x^2 + 6y^2 = 24$ _____

25. $\dfrac{(x + 2)^2}{25} + \dfrac{(y - 3)^2}{9} = 1$ _____

26. $2(x + 3)^2 + 8(y - 2)^2 = 32$ _____

27. $x^2 + 4y^2 - 2x + 16y + 13 = 0$ _____

28. $9x^2 + 36x + y^2 - 6y + 9 = 0$ _____

10-4   For each hyperbola find the center, the vertices, the foci, and the asymptotes. Then draw a graph.

1. $\dfrac{x^2}{16} - \dfrac{y^2}{4} = 1$ _____

2. $\dfrac{x^2}{4} - \dfrac{y^2}{16} = 1$ _____

3. $y^2 - x^2 = 4$ _____

4. $9y^2 - x^2 = 9$ _____

5. $\dfrac{(x-3)^2}{9} - \dfrac{(y+2)^2}{16} = 1$ _____

6. $\dfrac{(y+2)^2}{9} - \dfrac{(x+3)^2}{4} = 1$ _____

7. $x^2 - 2x - y^2 - 4y - 2 = 0$ _____

8. $4x^2 - 8x - y^2 + 4y - 4 = 0$ _____

10-4   Graph.

9. $xy = 2$ 10. $xy = -2$ 11. $xy = -5$

10-5   For each parabola find the vertex, the focus, and the directrix. Then draw a graph.

12. $y^2 = 2x$ _____   13. $y = -\dfrac{1}{2}x^2$ _____

14. $y^2 - 8x = 0$ _____   15. $x^2 + 8y = 0$ _____

10-5   Find an equation of a parabola with vertex at the origin satisfying the given condition.

16. focus $(2, 0)$ _____   17. focus $\left(0, \dfrac{1}{2}\right)$ _____

18. focus $(0, -\sqrt{2})$ _____   19. focus $(-3, 0)$ _____

10-5   Find the vertex, the focus, and the directrix. Then draw a graph.

20. $x^2 = 2(y - 4)$ _____

21. $y^2 = 6(x + 2)$ _____

22. $(x + 1)^2 = -8(y - 3)$ _____

23. $(y + 2)^2 = 4(x - 1)$ _____

24. $x^2 - 4y + 16 = 0$ _____

25. $4x = y^2 + 2y + 5$ _____

10-6   Tell which conic is defined by each equation.

1. $3x^2 + 4x + 2y + 6 = 0$ _____

2. $3x^2 + 4x - 5y^2 + 1 = 0$ _____

3. $3x^2 + 5y^2 - 2 = 0$ _____

4. $-3x^2 - 5y^2 + 2 = 0$ _____

5. $-2x^2 + 4x + y^2 - y = 0$ _____

6. $7x^2 + 7y^2 = 1$ _____

10-6   Solve each system graphically.

7. $x^2 + y^2 = 25$
$4y = 3x$

8. $x^2 = y + 2$
$y + 2 = 2x$

9. $xy = 8$
$y = x + 2$

10-6   Solve.

10. $y^2 - x^2 = 16$
$y + 3x = -4$ _____

11. $4x^2 + 9y^2 = 36$
$3y + 2x = -6$ _____

12. $2x^2 + xy = 8$
$y = 2x + 4$ _____

13. $x^2 + 4y^2 = 4$
$2y + 2 = x$ _____

10-7   Solve each system graphically. Then solve algebraically.

14. $y = x^2 + 1$
$y + x^2 = 3$ _____

15. $9x^2 + y^2 = 9$
$x^2 + y^2 = 9$ _____

16. $x^2 - y^2 = 4$
$x^2 + y^2 = 4$ _____

10-7   Solve.

17. $xy = 12$
$x^2 + y^2 = 40$ _____

18. $x^2 + y^2 = 15$
$2x^2 - y^2 = 18$ _____

19. $x^2 + 2y^2 = 18$
$x^2 + y^2 = 10$ _____

10-8   Solve.

20. A rectangular park has a perimeter of 14 km and is 5 km from opposite corners. Find the length of each side of the park.

_____

21. The area of a ping-pong table is 45 ft^2 and the length of a diagonal is $\sqrt{106}$ ft. Find the dimensions.

_____

11-1   Determine whether the given numbers are roots of the polynomial equation $P(x) = 0$.

1. $P(x) = x^3 + 2x^2 - 5x - 6$
  a. -1 _____   **b.** 2 _____

2. $P(x) = x^3 + 3x^2 + x + 3$
  a. 1 _____   **b.** -3 _____

11-1   Determine whether the given numbers are zeros of the polynomial functions.

3. $P(x) = 2x^3 + x^2 + 4x + 2$
  a. $i\sqrt{2}$ _____   **b.** $-i\sqrt{2}$ _____

4. $P(x) = x^3 - 2x^2 + x - 2$
  a. i _____   **b.** -2 _____

11-1   Divide to determine whether the monomials are factors of the polynomial $P(x)$.

5. $P(x) = x^3 - 2x^2 + x - 2$
  a. $x - 2$ _____   **b.** $x - 1$ _____

6. $P(x) = x^3 - 5x^2 + 7x - 2$
  a. $x + 1$ _____   **b.** $x + 2$ _____

11-1   Divide each $P(x)$ by $D(x)$. Then express the dividend as $P(x) = D(x) \cdot Q(x) + R(x)$.

7. $P(x) = x^3 + 3x^2 - 4x + 1$
  $D(x) = x + 1$ _____

8. $P(x) = x^4 - x^3 - 2x + 4$
  $D(x) = x - 2$ _____

11-2   Find the function values.

9. $P(x) = x^3 - 2x^2 + x$
  a. $P(-2)$ _____   **b.** $P(1)$ _____

10. $P(x) = x^4 + x^3 - 4x^2 + 3$
  a. $P(-2)$ _____   **b.** $P(-1)$ _____

11-2   Determine whether the numbers are roots of the polynomials.

11. $P(x) = x^3 + 3x^2 + x + 3$; i _____, 2 _____

12. $P(x) = x^3 - x^2 + 4x - 4$; 1 _____, -2 _____

11-2   Determine whether the expressions of the type $x - r$ are factors of the polynomial $P(x)$.

13. $P(x) = 3x^3 + 9x^2 - 11x + 4$; $x + 4$ _____

14. $P(x) = 3x^4 - 8x^3 + 9x + 5$; $x - 2$ _____

15. Let $P(x) = x^3 - 2x^2 - x + 2$.
  a. Determine whether $x - 1$ is a factor of $P(x)$. _____
  b. Find a complete factorization of $P(x)$. _____
  c. Solve the equation $P(x) = 0$. _____

11-2   Factor the polynomial $P(x)$. Then solve the equation $P(x) = 0$.

16. $P(x) = x^3 + x^2 - 4x - 4$ _____

17. $P(x) = x^4 + x^3 - 7x^2 - x + 6$ _____

11-3   Find the roots of each polynomial equation, and state the multiplicity of each root.

    1. $P(x) = (x - 2)^3(x + 7)^4$ _____

11-3   Find a polynomial of degree 3 with the given numbers as roots.

    2. 1, 2, 3 _____   **3.** $1, i, -i$ _____

    4. $1 + i, 1 - i, -2$ _____   **5.** $-1, -2, -3$ _____

    6. Find a polynomial of degree 5 with 1 as a root of multiplicity 3 and -4 as a root of multiplicity 2. _____

11-3   Suppose a polynomial of degree 5 with rational coefficients has the given roots. Find all roots of the polynomial.

    7. $1, -2, 3, -4 + 5i$ _____   **8.** $1, 2 + \sqrt{3}, 6i$ _____

11-3   Find a polynomial of lowest degree with rational coefficients that has the given numbers as some of its roots.

    9. $2i, 2$ _____   **10.** $\sqrt{2}, -5$ _____

    11. $2 + \sqrt{2}, -3$ _____   **12.** $1 - i, 2$ _____

11-3   Given that the polynomial has the given root, find all roots of the polynomial.

    13. $P(x) = x^3 + 3x^2 + 4x + 12; -3$ _____

    14. $P(x) = x^4 - x^3 - x^2 - x - 2; i$ _____

    15. $P(x) = x^4 + x^3 - x^2 + x - 2; i$ _____

11-4   Find the rational roots, if they exist, of each polynomial. Find the other roots, if possible.

    16. $P(x) = 2x^3 - 5x^2 + x + 2$ _____

    17. $P(x) = 2x^3 - 3x^2 - 7x - 6$ _____

    18. $P(x) = x^3 - x^2 - 3x + 3$ _____

11-4   Find only the rational roots.

    19. $P(x) = x^3 + 5x^2 - x - 5$ _____

    20. $P(x) = x^4 + 3x^3 + 6x^2 + 12x + 8$ _____

    21. $P(x) = x^4 + 3x^3 - 3x^2 - 15x - 10$ _____

11-5   Use Descartes' rule of signs to determine the number of positive real roots.

1. $P(x) = 3x^6 + 4x^3 + x + 1$ _____   **2.** $P(x) = x^4 + 2x^3 - x^2 + x + 1$ _____

3. $P(x) = 4x^5 - x^3 + x^2 - x - 2$ _____   **4.** $P(x) = 3x^7 - x^5 + x^3 - x + 3$ _____

5. $P(x) = x^9 - x^5 + x^3 + 1$ _____   **6.** $P(x) = x^{21} + x^{10} - x^8 + x^3 + 5$ _____

7. $P(x) = 3x^{20} - 2x^6 + x^4 - 4$ _____   **8.** $P(x) = 3x^9 + 2x^5 - x^4 + 5x - 1$ _____

11-5   Use Descartes' rule of signs to determine the number of negative real roots.

9. $P(x) = 3x^6 + 4x^3 + x + 1$ _____   **10.** $P(x) = x^4 + 2x^3 - x^2 + x + 1$ _____

11. $P(x) = 4x^5 - x^3 + x^2 - x - 2$ _____   **12.** $P(x) = 3x^7 - x^5 + x^3 - x + 3$ _____

13. $P(x) = x^9 - x^5 + x^3 + 1$ _____   **14.** $P(x) = x^{21} + x^{10} - x^8 + x^3 + 5$ _____

15. $P(x) = 3x^{20} - 2x^6 + x^4 - 4$ _____   **16.** $P(x) = 3x^9 + 2x^5 - x^4 + 5x - 1$ _____

11-6   Graph.

17. $P(x) = x^3 - 2x^2 + 4$ _____   **18.** $P(x) = x^3 - 2x^2 + 1$ _____

19. $P(x) = x^3 - 2x + 1$ _____   **20.** $P(x) = x^3 - 2x - 1$ _____

21. $P(x) = x^4 - x^3 - 7x^2 + x + 7$ _____   **22.** $P(x) = x^5 - 4x^3 + x^2 + 3x - 1$ _____

11-6   Graph each polynomial. Find approximate roots to the nearest tenth.

23. $P(x) = x^3 - 4x - 3$ _____   **24.** $P(x) = x^3 - 4x + 3$ _____

25. $P(x) = x^3 - 2x^2 - 7x + 8$ _____   **26.** $P(x) = x^3 + x^2 - 7x + 4$ _____

27. $P(x) = x^3 - 2x^2 - 6x + 7$ _____   **28.** $P(x) = x^3 + x^2 - 8x - 8$ _____

29. $P(x) = x^4 + x^3 - 5x^2 - 2x + 4$ _____

30. $P(x) = x^4 - x^3 - 5x^2 + 3x + 4$ _____

31. $P(x) = x^4 + 5x^3 + 5x^2 - 5x - 6$ _____

32. $P(x) = x^5 + x^4 - x^3 + x^2 - x - 1$ _____

33. $P(x) = x^5 + x^4 - x^3 + 2x^2 - 2x - 4$ _____

SKILLS PRACTICE 33

For use with Lessons 12-1 through 12-3

NAME _____

DATE _____

12-1 Find the inverse of the following relations.

1. $\{(2, 7), (-1, -2), (3, -4)\}$ _____ **2.** $\{(-10, -10), (6, -1)\}$ _____

12-1 Test for symmetry with respect to the line $y = x$.

3. $4x + 4y = 9$ _____ **4.** $x^2 + y^2 = 4$ _____ **5.** $y = -3x^2$ _____

6. $4x^2 + 9y^2 = 36$ _____ **7.** $x = |3y|$ _____ **8.** $2x = \dfrac{3}{y}$ _____

12-1 Find equations for $f^{-1}(x)$ for the following.

9. $f(x) = 3x - 5$ _____ **10.** $f(x) = -x - 6$ _____

11. $f(x) = 0.4x + 3$ _____ **12.** $f(x) = x + 8$ _____

13. $f(x) = \sqrt{x + 2}$ _____ **14.** $f(x) = 4x + 1$ _____

15. $f(x) = 2x - 1$ _____ **16.** $f(x) = 2\sqrt{x + 3}$ _____

12-2 Graph. Where possible, use transformations.

17. $y = 3^x$ _____ **18.** $y = (0.5)^x$ _____

19. $y = \log_6 x$ _____ **20.** $y = \log_{0.5} x$ _____

12-3 Convert to logarithmic equations.

21. $3^4 = 81$ _____ **22.** $25^{\frac{1}{2}} = 5$ _____

23. $9^{\frac{3}{2}} = 27$ _____ **24.** $x^{-y} = z$ _____

12-3 Convert to exponential equations.

25. $\log_4 4 = 1$ _____ **26.** $\log_2 64 = 6$ _____

27. $\log_{10} 0.001 = -3$ _____ **28.** $\log_{10} 2 = 0.3010$ _____

29. $\log_3 \sqrt{3} = \dfrac{1}{2}$ _____ **30.** $\log_4 8 = \dfrac{3}{2}$ _____

12-3 Solve.

31. $\log_4 x = 3$ _____ **32.** $\log_x 125 = 3$ _____ **33.** $\log_x 6 = \dfrac{1}{3}$ _____

34. $\log_6 x = 3$ _____ **35.** $\log_9 x = \dfrac{3}{2}$ _____ **36.** $\log_x 27 = \dfrac{3}{4}$ _____

Simplify.

37. $2^{\log_2 8}$ _____ **38.** $\log_a a^3$ _____ **39.** $\log_b b^c$ _____

12-4   Express as a sum of logarithms. Simplify, if possible.

1. $\log_3 (9 \cdot 81)$ _____   **2.** $\log_2 (4 \cdot 8)$ _____

3. $\log_b 7y$ _____   **4.** $\log_t Dx$ _____

12-4   Express as a product.

5. $\log_a x^4$ _____   **6.** $\log_c t^6$ _____   **7.** $\log_b y^3$ _____

12-4   Express as a difference of logarithms.

8. $\log_a \dfrac{45}{2}$ _____   **9.** $\log_b \dfrac{B}{5}$ _____

12-4   Express in terms of logarithms of x, y, and z.

10. $\log_a 4xy^2z^4$ _____   **11.** $\log_a \dfrac{x^2y}{z^3}$ _____

12. $\log_a \sqrt[3]{\dfrac{x}{yz^2}}$ _____   **13.** $\log_b 7x^3yz^2$ _____

12-4   Express as a single logarithm. Simplify, if possible.

14. $\log_a x^3 + 3 \log_a y$ _____   **15.** $\dfrac{1}{3} \log_a x - 2 \log_a y + 2 \log_a x$ _____

16. $\log_a 2x + 2 \log_a \sqrt{x}$ _____   **17.** $\log_a (x^2 - 9) - \log_a (x + 3)$ _____

12-4   Given $\log_{10} 2 \approx 0.301$ and $\log_{10} 5 \approx 0.699$, find the following.

18. $\log_{10} 25$ _____   **19.** $\log_{10} \dfrac{1}{2}$ _____   **20.** $\log_{10} \sqrt{\dfrac{2}{5}}$ _____

21. $\log_{10} 20$ _____   **22.** $\log_{10} \sqrt[3]{5}$ _____   **23.** $\log_{10} 8$ _____

12-5   Use a calculator or Table 2 to find these logarithms.

24. $\log 6.15$ _____   **25.** $\log 1.97$ _____   **26.** $\log 5.67$ _____

27. $\log 8.63$ _____   **28.** $\log 456$ _____   **29.** $\log 89.5$ _____

30. $\log 0.27$ _____   **31.** $\log 0.00159$ _____   **32.** $\log 0.052$ _____

12-5   Use a calculator or Table 2 to find these antilogarithms.

33. antilog 0.8432 _____   **34.** antilog 0.7067 _____   **35.** antilog 0.9777 _____

36. antilog 2.4378 _____   **37.** antilog 1.1847 _____   **38.** antilog 4.3927 _____

39. antilog $(6.6222 - 10)$ _____   **40.** antilog $(9.0334 - 10)$ _____

SKILLS PRACTICE 35
For use with Lessons 12-7 through 12-8

NAME _____

DATE _____

12-7   Solve.

1. $2^x = 64$ _____   **2.** $3^x = 243$ _____   **3.** $3^{2x+3} = 81$ _____

4. $5^{3x} = 125$ _____   **5.** $8^x = 4$ _____   **6.** $2^x = \dfrac{1}{8}$ _____

7. $3^x = 5^{x-1}$ _____   **8.** $(54)^{3x} = 19$ _____   **9.** $(7.4)^x = 18.6$ _____

12-7   Solve.

10. $\log_3 (2x + 5) = 2$ _____   **11.** $\log_5 (4x - 1) = 3$ _____

12. $\log \sqrt{x^2 - 1} = 2$ _____   **13.** $\log (x + 9) - \log x = 1$ _____

14. $\log_2 x + \log_2 (x + 3) = 2$ _____   **15.** $\log_6 x + \log_6 (x + 5) = 2$ _____

12-7   Solve.

16. How many years will it take an investment of $1000 to double itself when interest is compounded annually at 4%?

_____

17. Find the loudness in decibels of the sound of a tractor having an intensity of 7,400,000 times I_0.

_____

12-8   Graph.

18. $y = e^{x\sqrt{3}}$

19. $y = e^{-x\sqrt{3}}$

12-8   Find each natural logarithm. Use a calculator or Table 3.

20. ln 4.32 _____   **21.** ln 43.2 _____   **22.** ln 432 _____

23. ln 0.432 _____   **24.** ln 8700 _____   **25.** ln 93,000 _____

12-8   Solve.

26. The approximate population of Albuquerque was 330,000 in 1980. In 1985 it was 370,000. Estimate the population in the year 2000.

_____

27. The half-life of a lead isotope is 22 years. After 88 years, how much of a 2000-gram sample will remain as the original isotope?

_____

12-8   Use common (base 10) logarithms to find the following.

28. $\log_6 25$ _____   **29.** $\log_5 0.27$ _____   **30.** $\log_8 39$ _____

31. $\log_{11} 14,000$ _____   **32.** ln 14 _____   **33.** ln 0.52 _____

13-1   Find the dimensions of each matrix.

1. $\begin{bmatrix} 3 & -7 \\ 8 & 5 \\ 0 & 1 \end{bmatrix}$
_____

2. $[10]$

3. $\begin{bmatrix} 2 & -1 & -3 & 8 \\ 5 & 0 & -4 & 4 \end{bmatrix}$
_____

4. $[3 \quad 2 \quad 8 \quad -4]$

5. $\begin{bmatrix} 2 \\ 0 \\ -5 \end{bmatrix}$
_____

6. $\begin{bmatrix} 7 & -1 & 0 \\ 2 & -4 & 3 \end{bmatrix}$
_____

13-1   Solving using matrices.

7. $3x + 2y = 12$
$4x - y = 5$ _____

8. $5x + 2y = -4$
$3x - 3y = 6$ _____

9. $2x - 5y = -3$
$x + y = -5$ _____

10. $2x + 4 = 3y$
$x - 2y + 4 = 0$ _____

11. $4x - y = -1$
$x + 3y = 16$ _____

12. $x + 5y = 2$
$2x - y = -7$ _____

13. $3x + 4y - z = 7$
$x - 2y + 4z = -2$
$2x + 3y + 2z = 2$ _____

14. $2x - y + 2z = 9$
$x + 2y + 3z = 8$
$3x + y - z = -1$ _____

15. $x + y + z = 1$
$2x + 3y - z = 3$
$x - 2y + 4z = 4$ _____

13-2   Add.

16. $\begin{bmatrix} 2 & -1 \\ 0 & 3 \end{bmatrix} + \begin{bmatrix} 5 & -4 \\ -2 & -1 \end{bmatrix}$ _____

17. $\begin{bmatrix} 6 & 1 \\ -3 & 1 \end{bmatrix} + \begin{bmatrix} 2 & 0 \\ -1 & -4 \end{bmatrix}$ _____

18. $\begin{bmatrix} 4 & 5 \\ -4 & -2 \end{bmatrix} + \begin{bmatrix} 0 & 0 \\ 0 & 0 \end{bmatrix}$ _____

19. $\begin{bmatrix} 5 & 2 & 0 \\ -3 & -1 & 2 \\ 1 & 4 & -1 \end{bmatrix} + \begin{bmatrix} 0 & -2 & 0 \\ 4 & -2 & -3 \\ 3 & -2 & -1 \end{bmatrix}$ _____

13-2   Find the additive inverse of each matrix.

20. $\begin{bmatrix} 5 & 2 & 1 \\ -2 & -1 & 4 \end{bmatrix}$ _____

21. $\begin{bmatrix} 3 & 0 & 1 \\ -1 & -1 & 2 \\ 2 & -4 & -3 \end{bmatrix}$ _____

13-2   Subtract.

22. $\begin{bmatrix} 4 & 2 \\ 1 & -1 \end{bmatrix} - \begin{bmatrix} 3 & -2 \\ 1 & -3 \end{bmatrix}$ _____

23. $\begin{bmatrix} 0 & 1 \\ 2 & 0 \end{bmatrix} - \begin{bmatrix} 3 & -3 \\ 2 & 2 \end{bmatrix}$ _____

24. $\begin{bmatrix} 4 & 0 & -3 \\ 2 & -1 & 5 \end{bmatrix} - \begin{bmatrix} -2 & -1 & 4 \\ -3 & -1 & 2 \end{bmatrix}$ _____

25. $\begin{bmatrix} 4 & 0 & 2 \\ 1 & -1 & 0 \\ -2 & 3 & 5 \end{bmatrix} - \begin{bmatrix} 2 & 0 & 2 \\ 1 & -3 & -2 \\ 2 & 1 & 3 \end{bmatrix}$ _____

SKILLS PRACTICE 37

For use with Lessons 13-3 through 13-4

NAME _____

DATE _____

13-3   Evaluate.

1. $\begin{vmatrix} 4 & 3 \\ 2 & 5 \end{vmatrix}$ _____

2. $\begin{vmatrix} -1 & 2 \\ 6 & 2 \end{vmatrix}$ _____

3. $\begin{vmatrix} 3 & 0 \\ -2 & -2 \end{vmatrix}$ _____

4. $\begin{vmatrix} 5.2 & 4.1 \\ 2.5 & 1.3 \end{vmatrix}$ _____

5. $\begin{vmatrix} -3 & 4 \\ -3 & 4 \end{vmatrix}$ _____

6. $\begin{vmatrix} 2 & -6 \\ -1 & -3 \end{vmatrix}$ _____

13-3   Solve using Cramer's rule.

7. $3x - y = 1$
$4x - 3y = 2$ _____

8. $3x + 4y = 0$
$x - 2y = 0$ _____

9. $x - y = -4$
$2x + 4y = 7$ _____

13-3   Evaluate.

10. $\begin{vmatrix} 0 & 1 & 0 \\ 3 & -2 & 4 \\ -1 & -3 & 2 \end{vmatrix}$ _____

11. $\begin{vmatrix} 2 & -1 & -1 \\ 0 & 3 & -2 \\ 0 & 3 & 4 \end{vmatrix}$ _____

12. $\begin{vmatrix} 1 & 2 & -1 \\ 3 & -1 & 2 \\ -2 & 1 & -3 \end{vmatrix}$ _____

13-3   Solve using Cramer's rule.

13. $3x - 4y + z = 5$
$x + 3y - 2z = -1$
$2x - y + 2z = 9$ _____

14. $x - 2y - z = 3$
$3x + 4y - 2z = 2$
$-2x + y + 3z = 0$ _____

15. $2x + y - 2z = 3$
$x - 3y + z = 4$
$3x + 4y + 2z = 4$ _____

13-4   Find each product, if possible.

16. $(-1)\begin{bmatrix} -2 & 5 \\ 7 & -3 \end{bmatrix}$ _____

17. $\begin{bmatrix} 2 & -3 & 1 \end{bmatrix}\begin{bmatrix} 4 \\ -1 \\ 2 \end{bmatrix}$ _____

18. $\begin{bmatrix} 3 & -4 \\ 1 & 2 \end{bmatrix}\begin{bmatrix} 2 & -3 \\ -1 & 4 \end{bmatrix}$ _____

19. $\begin{bmatrix} 2 & 0 \\ 3 & -4 \end{bmatrix}\begin{bmatrix} 5 & 1 \\ 1 & -2 \end{bmatrix}$ _____

20. $\begin{bmatrix} 5 & 1 \\ 2 & 4 \end{bmatrix}\begin{bmatrix} 2 \\ 0 \\ -3 \end{bmatrix}$ _____

21. $\begin{bmatrix} 2 & 1 \\ 4 & -3 \\ 0 & 2 \end{bmatrix}\begin{bmatrix} 3 \\ -2 \end{bmatrix}$ _____

22. $\begin{bmatrix} 5 & 0 & 2 \\ -1 & -1 & 3 \\ 4 & -2 & 1 \end{bmatrix}\begin{bmatrix} 2 & -1 & 1 \\ 3 & 3 & 1 \\ 0 & -2 & 4 \end{bmatrix}$ _____

13-4   Write a matrix equation equivalent to the following system of equations.

23. $3x + 2y - 3z + w = 0$
$2x - y + 4z + 3w = 5$
$-x - z + 2w = 8$
$3x + 10y + z = 6$ _____

13-5   Determine whether A and B are inverses.

1.
$$A = \begin{bmatrix} 3 & 2 \\ -1 & 4 \end{bmatrix} \quad B = \begin{bmatrix} \frac{2}{7} & -\frac{1}{7} \\ \frac{1}{14} & \frac{3}{14} \end{bmatrix}$$ _____

2.
$$A = \begin{bmatrix} 1 & 3 \\ 4 & 2 \end{bmatrix} \quad B = \begin{bmatrix} \frac{1}{10} & -\frac{2}{5} \\ -\frac{3}{10} & \frac{1}{5} \end{bmatrix}$$ _____

13-5   Find A^{-1}, if it exists. Check your answers by calculating AA^{-1} and $A^{-1}A$.

3. $\begin{bmatrix} 2 & 1 \\ 5 & 3 \end{bmatrix}$ _____

4. $\begin{bmatrix} 0 & -3 \\ 3 & 0 \end{bmatrix}$ _____

5. $\begin{bmatrix} 7 & 2 \\ 5 & 3 \end{bmatrix}$ _____

6. $\begin{bmatrix} 4 & 3 \\ -5 & -4 \end{bmatrix}$ _____

7. $\begin{bmatrix} 5 & 1 \\ 10 & 2 \end{bmatrix}$ _____

8. $\begin{bmatrix} 1 & 0 \\ 0 & 3 \end{bmatrix}$ _____

13-6   Find A^{-1}, if it exists.

9. $\begin{bmatrix} 1 & 2 & 3 \\ 1 & 1 & 2 \\ -1 & 2 & 2 \end{bmatrix}$ _____

10. $\begin{bmatrix} 1 & 0 & 2 \\ 1 & 1 & 1 \\ 3 & -2 & 1 \end{bmatrix}$ _____

11. $\begin{bmatrix} 3 & 2 & 1 \\ 0 & 0 & 0 \\ -1 & 1 & 2 \end{bmatrix}$ _____

12. $\begin{bmatrix} 1 & 2 & 1 \\ 0 & 1 & 2 \\ -3 & 0 & 1 \end{bmatrix}$ _____

13. $\begin{bmatrix} 4 & 2 & 1 \\ 8 & 4 & 2 \\ 1 & 3 & 1 \end{bmatrix}$ _____

14. $\begin{bmatrix} 1 & 2 & 3 \\ 3 & 4 & 1 \\ -1 & 0 & 2 \end{bmatrix}$ _____

13-6   Solve using matrices.

15. $8x - 7y = 10$
$5x + 3y = 21$ _____

16. $4x + 3y = 4$
$x + 2y = 6$ _____

17. $3x - 2y = 11$
$5x + y = 1$ _____

18. $3x - y = 5$
$6x - 2y = 10$ _____

19. $x - 2y = 1$
$2x + 5z = 5$
$x + y - z = 8$ _____

20. $5x - 4y - z = -1$
$3x + y - 3z = 0$
$-2x + y + z = 4$ _____

13-7   Solve.

21. During one month a toymaker sells wooden bears and lions to three outlets in the following quantities.

	Outlet		
	A	B	C
Bears	25	15	18
Lions	14	10	17

The toymaker receives a profit of $3.50 for each bear sold and $4.00 for each lion. Find the profit the toymaker receives from each outlet.

_____

22. John and Mary received the following numbers of grades one semester.

	Grades			
	As	Bs	Cs	Ds
John	1	2	2	1
Mary	2	2	1	1

Students receive 4 points per A, 3 per B, 2 per C, and 1 per D. Find the total number of points each student received.

_____

14-1 The general term of a sequence is given. Find the 12th term.

1. $a_n = 4n + 3$ _____ **2.** $a_n = n - \dfrac{1}{n}$ _____ **3.** $a_n = (-1)^n 2^{n-7}$ _____

14-1 For each sequence find a general term.

4. $\sqrt{3}, \sqrt{6}, \sqrt{9}, \sqrt{12}, \sqrt{15}, \ldots$ _____

5. $\dfrac{2}{1}, \dfrac{3}{2}, \dfrac{4}{3}, \dfrac{5}{4}, \dfrac{6}{5}, \ldots$ _____

6. $-2, 5, -8, 11, -14, \ldots$ _____

7. $\log 1, \log 2, \log 4, \log 8, \log 16, \ldots$ _____

14-1 Find S_2 and S_4 for each sequence.

8. $1, 10, 100, 1000, 10{,}000, \ldots$ _____ **9.** $3, 6, 9, 12, 15, \ldots$ _____

14-1 Rename and evaluate each sum.

10. $\displaystyle\sum_{n=1}^{5} \dfrac{1}{3}n$ _____ **11.** $\displaystyle\sum_{n=3}^{6} \sqrt{2n+3}$ _____

14-1 Write sigma notation for each sum.

12. $1 + 4 + 7 + 10 + 13$ _____

13. $\dfrac{1}{4} - \dfrac{1}{9} + \dfrac{1}{16} - \dfrac{1}{25} + \dfrac{1}{36} - \dfrac{1}{49}$ _____

14-2 Find the specified term of the given arithmetic sequences.

14. 10th term of $3, 5, 7, \ldots$ _____ **15.** 12th term of $0.16, 0.11, 0.06, \ldots$ _____

14-2 In the given sequences, what term has the specified value?

16. $1, 4, 7, \ldots$; 34 _____ **17.** $0.03, 0.07, 0.11, \ldots$; 0.51 _____

14-2 Insert three arithmetic means between each pair of numbers.

18. 8 and 28 _____ **19.** 2 and 14 _____ **20.** 10 and 34 _____

14-2 Find the sum of the numbers described.

21. The even numbers from 4 to 40, inclusive

22. The odd numbers from 1 to 111, inclusive

_____

_____

14-2 Find the sum of each series.

23. $\displaystyle\sum_{n=1}^{12} (2n - 5)$ _____ **24.** $\displaystyle\sum_{n=1}^{20} 4n$ _____ **25.** $\displaystyle\sum_{n=1}^{18} n$ _____

14-3   Find the common ratio for each geometric sequence.

1. $2, -4, 8, -16, \ldots$ _____

2. $14, 7, \dfrac{7}{2}, \dfrac{7}{4}, \ldots$ _____

3. $x, x^3, x^5, x^7, \ldots$ _____

4. $3, \dfrac{6}{m}, \dfrac{12}{m^2}, \dfrac{24}{m^3}, \ldots$ _____

14-3   Find the specified term of the given geometric sequence.

5. $1, 2, 4, \ldots$; 8th _____

6. $\dfrac{125}{16}, \dfrac{25}{8}, \dfrac{5}{4}, \ldots$; 6th _____

7. $2, -6, 18, \ldots$; 5th _____

8. $2, 2\sqrt{5}, 10, \ldots$; 10th _____

14-3   Insert two geometric means between each pair of numbers.

9. 16 and $\dfrac{1}{4}$ _____

10. -3 and -0.003 _____

11. 9 and 243 _____

14-3   Solve.

12. A college student borrowed $1200 at 16% interest compounded monthly. The loan is paid in one lump sum at the end of 3 years. How much will the student pay?

_____

13. A college student borrowed $500 at 12% interest compounded monthly. The loan is paid in one lump sum at the end of 2 years. How much will the student pay?

_____

14-3   Find the sum of the specified number of terms of the given geometric sequence.

14. $5 + 10 + 20 + \cdots$; first 9 terms _____

15. $\dfrac{1}{2} - \dfrac{1}{4} + \dfrac{1}{8} - \cdots$; first 7 terms _____

16. $27 - 9 + 3 - \cdots$; first 6 terms _____

17. $2 + 2\sqrt{5} + 10 + \cdots$; first 8 terms _____

18. $1 + \dfrac{1}{x} + \dfrac{1}{x^2} + \dfrac{1}{x^3} + \cdots$; first 8 terms _____

19. $1 + x^3 + x^6 + x^9 + \cdots$; first 10 terms _____

14-3   Find the sum of each geometric series.

20. $\displaystyle\sum_{k=1}^{8} \left(\dfrac{1}{2}\right)^{k-1}$ _____

21. $\displaystyle\sum_{k=1}^{4} 5^k$ _____

22. $\displaystyle\sum_{k=1}^{5} \left(\dfrac{1}{4}\right)^{k-1}$ _____

23. $\displaystyle\sum_{k=1}^{6} 3^{k-1}$ _____

24. $\displaystyle\sum_{k=1}^{7} \left(\dfrac{1}{2}\right)^{k}$ _____

25. $\displaystyle\sum_{k=1}^{5} 4^k$ _____

SKILLS PRACTICE 41

For use with Lessons 14-4 through 14-5

NAME _____

DATE _____

14-4 Determine which geometric series have sums.

1. $2 + 6 + 18 + 54 + \cdots$ _____

2. $20 + 10 + 5 + \dfrac{5}{2} + \cdots$ _____

3. $3 - 6 + 12 - 24 + \cdots$ _____

4. $5 + 0.5 + 0.05 + 0.005 + \cdots$ _____

5. $4 + 6 + 9 + \dfrac{27}{2} + \cdots$ _____

6. $1 - \dfrac{1}{4} + \dfrac{1}{16} - \dfrac{1}{64} + \cdots$ _____

7. $3 - 9 + 27 - 81 + \cdots$ _____

8. $8 + 2 + \dfrac{1}{2} + \dfrac{1}{8} + \cdots$ _____

14-4 Find the sum of each infinite geometric series.

9. $36 + 12 + 4 + \cdots$ _____

10. $6 + 5 + \dfrac{25}{6} + \cdots$ _____

11. $4 + 0.4 + 0.04 + \cdots$ _____

12. $\dfrac{8}{3} + \dfrac{4}{9} + \dfrac{2}{27} + \cdots$ _____

13. $6 + 2.4 + 0.96 + \cdots$ _____

14. $5 - 0.5 + 0.05 - \cdots$ _____

15. $\dfrac{3}{8} - \dfrac{3}{16} + \dfrac{3}{32} - \cdots$ _____

16. $18 + 1.8 + 0.18 + \cdots$ _____

17. $6 - 3 + \dfrac{3}{2} - \cdots$ _____

18. $\dfrac{7}{10} - \dfrac{7}{100} + \dfrac{7}{1000} - \cdots$ _____

19. $\dfrac{9}{5} + \dfrac{3}{5} + \dfrac{1}{5} + \cdots$ _____

20. $4 + 1 + \dfrac{1}{4} + \cdots$ _____

14-5 Use the principle of mathematical induction to prove each of the following.

21. $2 + 4 + 6 + \cdots + 2n = n(n + 1)$

22. $1 + 4 + 7 + \cdots + (3n - 2) = \dfrac{n}{2}(3n - 1)$

23. $3 + 3^2 + 3^3 + \cdots + 3^n = \dfrac{3}{2}(3^n - 1)$

24. $3 + 7 + 11 + \cdots + (4n - 1) = n(2n + 1)$

25. $2 + 7 + 12 + \cdots + (5n - 3) = \dfrac{n}{2}(5n - 1)$

26. $6 + 5 + 4 + \cdots + (7 - n) = \dfrac{1}{2}n(13 - n)$

27. $1 + \dfrac{1}{5} + \dfrac{1}{25} + \cdots + 5^{1-n} = \dfrac{5}{4}\left(1 - \left(\dfrac{1}{5}\right)^{n}\right)$

28. $1 \cdot 2 + 2 \cdot 3 + 3 \cdot 4 + \cdots + n(n + 1) = \dfrac{n(n + 1)(n + 2)}{3}$

29. $-4 - 7 - 10 - \cdots - (3n + 1) = -\dfrac{1}{2}n(3n + 5)$

15-1   Solve.

1. How many 6-letter code symbols can be formed with the letters *A, B, C, D, E,* and *F* without repetition? _____

2. How many 3-digit numbers can be formed using all the digits 6, 7, 8 with repetition allowed? _____

3. How many ways can 8 different cards be laid out on a table in a row? _____

4. A woman has 6 dogs, 4 cats, and 8 canaries. In how many ways can she select one of each species? _____

15-1   Evaluate.

5. $_7P_7$ _____   **6.** $_3P_3$ _____   **7.** 4! _____   **8.** 0! _____

15-1   Compute.

9. $_8P_6$ _____   **10.** $_{15}P_2$ _____   **11.** $_{10}P_6$ _____   **12.** $_9P_5$ _____

13. In how many ways can the letters of the set $\{S, T, U, L, G\}$ be arranged to form ordered codes of 4 letters without repetition? _____

14. How many 3-digit odd numbers can be formed from the digits 1, 2, 4, 6, 8, 9 if repetition is allowed? _____

15-2   Find the number of permutations of the letters of these words.

15. TROTTER _____

16. OFFICIAL _____

17. TOMORROW _____

18. CHEERLEADER _____

19. COLLECTION _____

20. LEVEL _____

15-2   Solve.

21. In how many ways can 3 blue flags, 3 white flags, and 2 green flags be arranged on a staff? _____

22. Find the number of permutations of eight people around a circular table.

_____

15-3   Simplify.

23. $\binom{10}{6}$ _____   **24.** $\binom{30}{2}$ _____   **25.** $\binom{15}{11}$ _____   **26.** $\binom{50}{3}$ _____

15-3   Solve.

27. There are 18 students in a club. How many ways can 5 officers be selected?

_____

28. How many lines are determined by 10 points, no 3 of which are collinear?

_____

SKILLS PRACTICE 43

For use with Lessons 15-4 through 15-6

15-4   Find the indicated term of the binomial expression.

1. 7th, $(x + y)^8$ _____

2. 4th, $(r + s)^9$ _____

3. 10th, $(x - 3)^{12}$ _____

4. 5th, $(a - 2)^{10}$ _____

5. Middle, $(3x - y)^8$ _____

6. Middle two, $(\sqrt{x} + \sqrt{2})^7$ _____

15-4   Expand.

7. $(x + y)^6$ _____

8. $(x - 2y^2)^4$ _____

9. $(2a - b)^5$ _____

10. $(\sqrt{3} + 1)^4$ _____

15-4   Determine the number of subsets of each of the following sets.

11. A set of 8 members _____

12. A set of 16 letters _____

15-5   Suppose we draw a card from a deck of 52 cards. What is the probability of drawing

13. a spade? _____

14. a 6? _____

15. a queen or a king? _____

16. a 7 or a 5? _____

15-5   Solve.

17. From a group of 8 dogs and 5 cats, 4 are chosen. What is the probability that 2 dogs and 2 cats are chosen?

_____

18. From a bag containing 5 nickels, 9 dimes, and 6 quarters, 7 coins are drawn at random all at once. What is the probability of getting 2 nickels, 3 dimes, and 2 quarters?

_____

15-6   Solve.

19. A bag contains four blue marbles, seven red marbles, and eight green marbles. One marble is drawn at random. What is the probability that it will be either blue or green?

_____

20. A die is rolled. What is the probability of rolling a prime number or a divisor of 6?

_____

21. A card is drawn from an ordinary deck of 52 cards. What is the probability that it will be a black card or a face card?

_____

22. A die is rolled twice. What is the probability of rolling a 4 on the first roll and an odd number on the second roll?

_____

16-1   Here are two sets of data. Construct a stem-and-leaf diagram for

1. the height in inches of children in a preschool.

36.2	33.7	37.1	33.9
36.4	34.0	35.5	37.5
33.6	34.7	36.5	37.2
34.5	36.9	37.8	35.8

2. the number of points scored by a basketball player during each game in a season.

18	8	22	14	3	0
29	31	14	20	7	9
33	28	19	13	6	10

16-1   Construct a frequency distribution showing the relative frequency for

3. the number of eggs 30 ducks laid in a year.

72	68	55	91	43	74	76	93
45	72	69	41	71	83	80	92
67	66	49	51	59	60	50	91
47	62	58	93	49	74		

4. the scores of 40 students on an exam.

85	100	90	82	76	64	55
71	86	93	79	80	62	43
91	83	75	94	87	67	76
45	98	84	85	71	78	78
88	63	57	100	97	81	73
71	84	87	92	95		

16-2   Here are two sets of data. For each set find the mean, the median, and the mode of

5. the number of cookies in 20 boxes of cookies.

Stem	Leaf
4	6, 5, 9, 4, 5
5	1, 3, 0, 4, 9, 4, 0, 5, 4
6	0, 5, 4, 4, 2, 3

mean _____

median _____

mode _____

6. the price of 15 books in a bookstore.

$3.95	$12.75	$21.25	$4.50	$29.35
$21.50	$3.95	$18.95	$15.50	$19.95
$23.50	$18.95	$3.95	$47.50	$14.95

mean _____

median _____

mode _____

16-3   Find the range, the mean deviation, the variance, and the standard deviation for

7. temperatures of 10 patients in a doctor's office.

98.5, 99.3, 101.7, 98.9, 99.9
103.1, 97.7, 99.0, 98.3, 104.7

range _____

mean deviation _____

variance _____

standard deviation _____

16-4   1. What is the z-score for 1150 in a normal distribution with a mean of 1225 and a standard deviation of 100? _____

A vocabulary test had results that were normally distributed with a mean score of 77.4 and a standard deviation of 7.2.

2. What percent of those tested scored 90 and above? _____

3. What percent of those tested scored 63 or below? _____

4. Of 4000 students, how many scored between 70 and 80? _____

16-5   5. Long High School has 1500 students, 75 of whom are members of the football team. Describe how to take a stratified random sample of 100 students. _____

16-6   6. A table of 100 random digits was generated by hand. Complete the table and calculate chi-square. _____

Outcome	Observed	Expected	Difference	Difference^2	$\dfrac{\text{Difference}^2}{\text{Expected}}$
0	5				
1	11				
2	6				
3	16				
4	10				
5	14				
6	7				
7	17				
8	8				
9	6				

7. Determine whether the above results occurred by chance. Test the null hypothesis at the 5% level of significance. _____

SKILLS PRACTICE 46

For use with Lessons 17-1 through 17-2

NAME _____

DATE _____

17-1 Find the indicated trigonometric function values for θ in each of the following triangles. Use rational notation.

1. Find sin θ, cos θ, and tan θ.

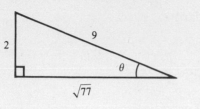

_____

2. Find sin θ, cos θ, and tan θ.

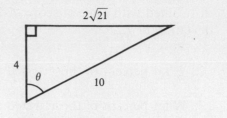

_____

3. Find sin θ, cos θ, and tan θ.

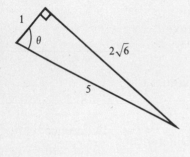

_____

4. Find sin θ, cos θ, and tan θ.

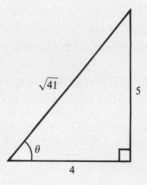

_____

17-1 Find the length of each labeled side.

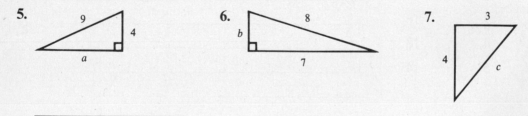

5.

6.

7.

_____ _____ _____

17-2 In which quadrant does the terminal side of each angle lie?

8. 63° _____ **9.** −192° _____ **10.** 363° _____ **11.** −89° _____

17-2 Find the reference angle for the following angles of rotation.

12. 405° _____ **13.** −120° _____ **14.** −330° _____ **15.** 270° _____

16. −300° _____ **17.** −90° _____ **18.** 120° _____ **19.** 750° _____

17-2 Find each of the following, or indicate those that are undefined.

20. cos 90° _____ **21.** tan 270° _____ **22.** cos 180° _____

23. tan 240° _____ **24.** sin −45° _____ **25.** tan −360° _____

17-3 ___ Convert to radian measure. Give answers in terms of π.

1. $-120°$ _____   **2.** $-60°$ _____   **3.** $135°$ _____   **4.** $150°$ _____

5. $-300°$ _____   **6.** $270°$ _____   **7.** $-90°$ _____   **8.** $45°$ _____

17-3 ___ Convert to degree measure.

9. $\dfrac{7\pi}{4}$ _____   **10.** $\dfrac{-\pi}{2}$ _____   **11.** $\dfrac{3\pi}{2}$ _____   **12.** π _____

13. $\dfrac{2\pi}{3}$ _____   **14.** $\dfrac{-\pi}{6}$ _____   **15.** $\dfrac{4\pi}{3}$ _____   **16.** $\dfrac{5\pi}{4}$ _____

17-4 ___ Use Table 5 to find the following.

17. $\cos 24°20'$ _____   **18.** $\sin 14°10'$ _____   **19.** $\tan 40°40'$ _____

20. $\csc 63°50'$ _____   **21.** $\cot 48°$ _____   **22.** $\cos 33°20'$ _____

23. $\tan 15°50'$ _____   **24.** $\sec 19°10'$ _____   **25.** $\sin 402°10'$ _____

26. $\cot 430°10'$ _____   **27.** $\sec 321°50'$ _____   **28.** $\cos -95°30'$ _____

29. $\csc 442°$ _____   **30.** $\sin 99°20'$ _____   **31.** $\cos 620°50'$ _____

17-5 ___ Which of the following functions are periodic?

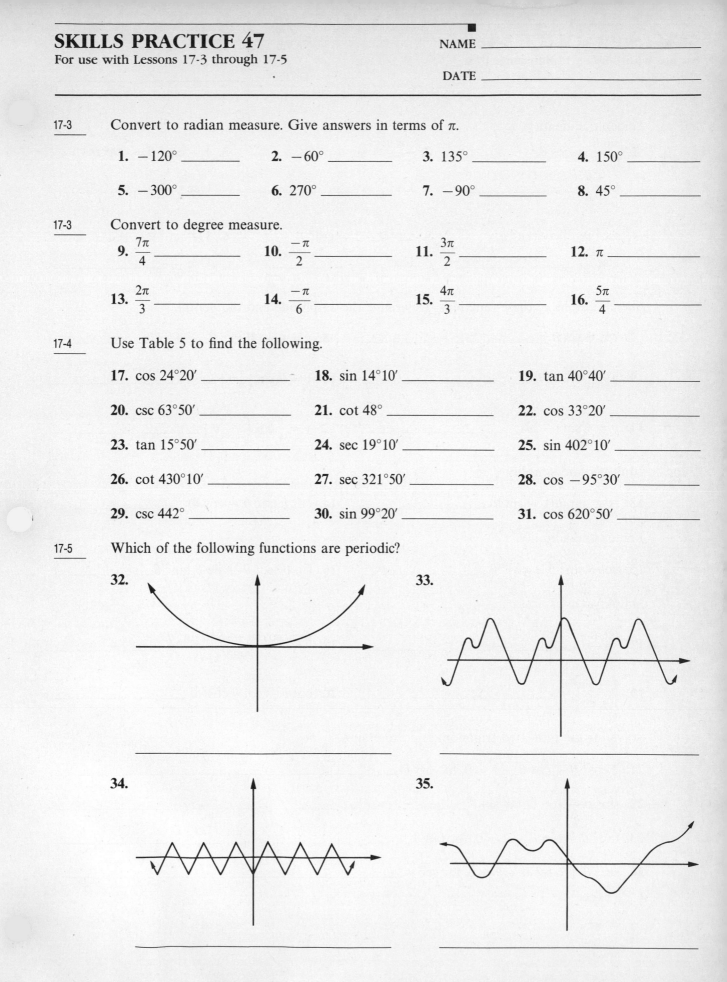

32.

_____

33.

_____

34.

_____

35.

_____

17-6   Check the identity.

1. $\dfrac{\sin \theta}{\tan \theta} = \cos \theta$

Use $\dfrac{\pi}{3}$. _____

2. $\dfrac{\cos \theta}{\cot \theta} = \sin \theta$

Use $\dfrac{\pi}{4}$. _____

3. $1 + \cot^2 \theta = \csc^2 \theta$

Use $\dfrac{\pi}{4}$. _____

4. $\sec^2 \theta - 1 = \tan^2 \theta$

Use $\dfrac{3\pi}{4}$. _____

5. $\csc^2 \theta - 1 = \cot^2 \theta$

Use $\dfrac{\pi}{2}$. _____

6. $1 + \tan^2 \theta = \sec^2 \theta$

Use $\dfrac{\pi}{6}$. _____

17-7   Sketch graphs of these functions. Determine the amplitude and the period.

7. $y = 3 \sin \theta$ _____

8. $y = \cos (4\theta)$ _____

9. $y = \dfrac{1}{3} \cos (3\theta)$ _____

10. $y = 7 \sin \left(\dfrac{1}{2}\theta\right)$ _____

11. $y = 4 \sin (-2\theta)$ _____

12. $y = \dfrac{1}{4} \cos \left(-\dfrac{1}{3}\theta\right)$ _____

17-8   Multiply and simplify.

13. $(1 + \sin \theta)(1 - \sin \theta)$ _____

14. $\cos \theta (\sec \theta - \cos \theta)$ _____

17-8   Factor and simplify.

15. $\cos \theta \sin^2 \theta + \cos^3 \theta$ _____

16. $\sin \theta \sec^2 \theta - \sin \theta \tan^2 \theta$ _____

17-8   Simplify.

17. $\dfrac{\tan \theta}{\sin \theta}$ _____

18. $\dfrac{\sec \theta \cos^2 \theta + \sec \theta \sin^2 \theta}{\csc \theta}$ _____

19. $\dfrac{1 - \sin^2 \theta}{1 - \cos^2 \theta}$ _____

20. $\cot \theta - \cot \theta \cos^2 \theta$ _____

17-8   Solve for the indicated trigonometric expression.

21. $2 \cos^2 \theta + \cos \theta - 1 = 0$, for $\cos \theta$ _____

22. $\sin^2 \theta - 1 = 0$, for $\sin \theta$ _____

23. $\tan^2 \theta - \tan \theta - 2 = 0$, for $\tan \theta$ _____

24. $\sec^2 \theta + 6 \sec \theta + 9 = 0$, for $\sec \theta$ _____

18-1   Use the sum and difference identities to simplify the following.

1. $\cos 20° \cos 25° - \sin 20° \sin 25°$ _____

2. $\cos 24° \cos (-6°) + \sin 24° \sin (-6°)$ _____

3. $\sin 8° \cos 22° + \cos 8° \sin 22°$ _____

4. $\sin 163° \cos 73° - \cos 163° \sin 73°$ _____

5. $\dfrac{\tan 28° + \tan 2°}{1 - \tan 28° \tan 2°}$ _____

6. $\dfrac{\tan 68° - \tan 23°}{1 + \tan 68° \tan 23°}$ _____

18-1   Use sum and difference formulas to find the following.

7. $\cos 22° \cos (-8°) + \sin 22° \sin (-8°)$ _____

8. $\cos 83° \cos 7° - \sin 83° \sin 7°$ _____

9. $\sin 48° \cos 3° - \cos 48° \sin 3°$ _____

10. $\dfrac{\tan 29° + \tan 16°}{1 - \tan 29° \tan 16°}$ _____

11. $\dfrac{\tan 69° - \tan 9°}{1 + \tan 69° \tan 9°}$ _____

18-2   Find $\sin 2\theta$, $\cos 2\theta$, $\tan 2\theta$, and the quadrant in which 2θ lies.

12. $\sin \theta = \dfrac{3}{5}$ (θ in quadrant I) _____

13. $\cos \theta = \dfrac{12}{13}$ (θ in quadrant IV) _____

14. $\cos \theta = \dfrac{5}{13}$ (θ in quadrant I) _____

15. $\sin \theta = \dfrac{3}{5}$ (θ in quadrant II) _____

18-2   Use Theorem 18-3 and Theorem 18-4 to find the following.

16. $\cos 15°$ _____

17. $\tan 15°$ _____

18. $\sin 22.5°$ _____

19. $\cos 22.5°$ _____

20. $\tan 75°$ _____

21. $\sin 75°$ _____

18-3   Prove these identities.

22. $\dfrac{\sin^3 \theta}{\cos \theta} + \sin \theta \cos \theta = \tan \theta$

23. $\dfrac{1}{\cos \theta \sin \theta} - \tan \theta = \cot \theta$

24. $\dfrac{1}{\cos \theta} - \cos \theta = \sin \theta \tan \theta$

25. $\sin \theta \tan \theta + \cos \theta = \sec \theta$

26. $\dfrac{\sin \theta \cos \theta}{1 - \cos^2 \theta} = \cot \theta$ _____

27. $\dfrac{\cot \theta \sec \theta \cos \theta \tan \theta}{\sin \theta} = \csc \theta$ _____

18-4   Find all values of the following.

1. arctan 1 _____   **2.** arccos 1 _____   **3.** arcsin -1 _____

4. $\sin^{-1} \frac{1}{2}$ _____   **5.** $\cos^{-1} 0$ _____   **6.** $\tan^{-1} \sqrt{3}$ _____

18-4   Find the following without using a table or a calculator.

7. $\text{Arcsin } \frac{1}{2}$ _____   **8.** Arctan 0 _____   **9.** $\text{Arccos } \frac{\sqrt{3}}{2}$ _____

10. Arcsin 0 _____   **11.** $\text{Tan}^{-1} 1$ _____   **12.** $\text{Sin}^{-1} \frac{\sqrt{3}}{2}$ _____

13. $\text{Cos}^{-1} \frac{1}{2}$ _____   **14.** $\text{Sin}^{-1} 1$ _____

18-5   Find all solutions to the following equations from 0 to 2π.

15. $\sin^2 \theta - 1 = 0$ _____   **16.** $\cos^2 \theta + \cos \theta + \frac{1}{4} = 0$ _____

17. $\tan^2 \theta + 2 \tan \theta + 1 = 0$ _____   **18.** $\sin^2 \theta - 2 \sin \theta + 1 = 0$ _____

19. $\cos^2 \theta + \sqrt{3} \cos \theta + \frac{3}{4} = 0$ _____   **20.** $\sin^2 \theta + \sin \theta = 0$ _____

21. $\tan^2 \theta - \tan \theta = 0$ _____   **22.** $\cos^2 \theta + \cos \theta = 0$ _____

23. $\cos^2 \theta + \frac{1 + \sqrt{3}}{2} \cos \theta + \frac{\sqrt{3}}{4} = 0$ _____

24. $\sin^2 \theta - \frac{1 + \sqrt{3}}{2} \sin \theta + \frac{\sqrt{3}}{4} = 0$ _____

18-6   In Exercises 25–31, standard lettering for a right triangle will be used. A, B, and C are the angles, C being the right angle. The sides opposite A, B, and C are a, b, and c, respectively. Solve the triangle using three-digit precision.

25. $m \angle A = 20$, $a = 6.3$ _____

26. $\angle A = 27°50'$, $a = 17$ _____

27. $\angle B = 16°50'$, $b = 26$ _____

28. $m \angle B = 19$, $a = 13$ _____

29. $\angle A = 9°50'$, $a = 44$ _____

30. $a = 6.4$, $c = 9$ _____

31. $b = 0.76$, $a = 43.7$ _____

18-7   Solve triangle ABC.

1. $m\angle A = 63, m\angle B = 14, b = 3$ _____

2. $m\angle B = 12, m\angle C = 73, c = 48$ _____

3. $\angle B = 21°, \angle A = 141°50', a = 93$ _____

4. $m\angle A = 47, m\angle B = 111, b = 19.4$ _____

5. $\angle B = 28°50', \angle C = 93°, a = 15$ _____

6. $m\angle C = 6, m\angle B = 87, a = 43.2$ _____

18-7   Find the area of triangle ABC.

7. $b = 11, c = 23, m\angle A = 64$ _____   **8.** $b = 21, c = 6, \angle A = 14°50'$ _____

9. $b = 2, c = 3, m\angle A = 100$ _____   **10.** $b = 7, c = 44, m\angle A = 69$ _____

18-8   Solve the triangles.

11. $m\angle A = 69, b = 4, c = 2$ _____

12. $m\angle B = 121, a = 9.7, c = 8$ _____

13. $m\angle B = 34, c = 19, a = 19$ _____

14. $m\angle C = 142, a = 101, b = 117.4$ _____

15. $a = 16, b = 50, c = 43$ _____

16. $a = 9, b = 6, c = 7$ _____

18-9   Find rectangular notation.

17. $7(\cos 90° + i \sin 90°)$ _____   **18.** $3(\cos 60° + i \sin 60°)$ _____

19. $13 \text{ cis } 120°$ _____   **20.** $43 \text{ cis } 150°$ _____

21. $2 \text{ cis } 300°$ _____   **22.** $4 \text{ cis } 210°$ _____

18-9   Find trigonometric notation.

23. $\sqrt{3} - i$ _____   **24.** $\sqrt{2} + i\sqrt{2}$ _____

25. $9i$ _____   **26.** $\dfrac{7}{2} + \dfrac{7\sqrt{3}}{2} i$ _____

27. 13 _____   **28.** 43 _____

Mixed Review Worksheets

The following 36 blackline masters are worksheets for extra practice in a mixed-review format. Each worksheet provides practice drawn from a variety of lessons in the student text. The appropriate time to distribute each worksheet is indicated at the top of the sheet. The lesson that each group of exercises has been modeled after is indicated in the left margin.

You will find these worksheets helpful for reviewing and reinforcing concepts with all of your students. They also can be incorporated within the context of a cumulative or semester review.

Simplify by performing the indicated operation.

1-1

1. $13 - (-15.2)$ _____

2. $-8.1 + (-4.3)$ _____

3. $5.8 - 17.7$ _____

4. $-\dfrac{2}{3} + \dfrac{2}{7}$ _____

5. $\dfrac{4}{7} - \left(-\dfrac{9}{7}\right)$ _____

6. $178 - (233)$ _____

7. $72 + (-41)$ _____

8. $-45 - (-63)$ _____

9. $-14.27 + (-11.74)$ _____

10. $-53.2 - (13.2)$ _____

1-2

11. $-\dfrac{1}{4} \div \left(-\dfrac{5}{12}\right)$ _____

12. $-\dfrac{16}{5}\left(-\dfrac{3}{7}\right)$ _____

13. $\left(-\dfrac{3}{4}\right)\left(-\dfrac{3}{4}\right)\left(-\dfrac{3}{4}\right)$ _____

14. $\dfrac{-9.6}{24}$ _____

Evaluate each expression.

1-3

15. $3y + 5x$ for $y = -2$, $x = 3$ _____

16. $4x - y$ for $x = -7$, $y = -9$ _____

17. $-y$ for $y = -\dfrac{2}{3}$ _____

18. $3|a - b|$ for $a = 4$, $b = 7$ _____

19. $9x - |x|$ for $x = 4$ _____

20. $6c - 3|d|$ for $c = 4$, $d = -4$ _____

Simplify.

1-4

21. $2\pi(r - h)$ _____

22. $7x(6y - z + 8w)$ _____

23. $5e(7f - 4g - h)$ _____

24. $5y - (3y + 6)$ _____

25. $4x - 3(y + 4x)$ _____

26. $14a + 3(x - a - 2)$ _____

27. $2(2x - 4y) - 3(x - 5y)$ _____

28. $-7(3m - 2y) - 3(7m + 5y)$ _____

Factor.

1-4

29. $9x + 9y$ _____

30. $5a - 15b - 5$ _____

31. $xy + 5x$ _____

32. $27x - 36$ _____

33. $4x - 20y - 36z$ _____

34. $abc + a$ _____

Determine whether the indicated number is a solution of the equation.

1-5

1. $4x + 7 = -5; -3$ _____

2. $9y - 14 = -4; 2$ _____

3. $7x + 37 = -9; -4$ _____

4. $5y - 15 = 0; -3$ _____

Solve.

1-5

5. $x + 14 = 4$ _____

6. $y - 17 = -6$ _____

7. $\frac{3}{7}y = -12$ _____

8. $-7.4x = -44.4$ _____

9. $7x - 10 = 11$ _____

10. $4y + 15 = 35$ _____

11. $3x - 7x = 28$ _____

12. $6x - x = -25$ _____

13. $4a = 3a + 7$ _____

14. $6a - 4 = 4a + 4$ _____

15. $4x - 100 = 15x + 21$ _____

16. $5y + y - 10 = 3y + 11$ _____

Multiply and simplify.

1-7

17. $5 \cdot 5 \cdot 5 \cdot 5 \cdot 5$ _____

18. $(3xy)(3xy)(3xy)$ _____

1-8

19. $11^5 \cdot 11^3$ _____

20. $7^{-5} \cdot 7^3$ _____

21. $y^4 \cdot y^{-7} \cdot y^4$ _____

22. $(4b^4c^{-3})(-3b^{-3}c^{-4})$ _____

23. $(5xy^6)(5x^4y^{-1})$ _____

24. $(x^4y^{-4})(x^3y^2)$ _____

Divide and simplify.

1-8

25. $\dfrac{x^5}{x^3}$ _____

26. $\dfrac{24x^{-5}y^{-6}}{-6x^{-10}y^{-4}}$ _____

27. $\dfrac{x^3}{x^5}$ _____

28. $\dfrac{5^{-4}a^8b^{-3}}{5^4a^{-2}b^2}$ _____

Simplify.

1-8

29. $(3^7)^4$ _____

30. $(2^{-6})^3$ _____

31. $(7^{-4})^{-3}$ _____

32. $(-2x^4y^{-5})^2$ _____

33. $(-3a^{-6}b^4)^{-3}$ _____

34. $\left(\dfrac{5x^3y^2}{11y^{-5}z^2}\right)^5$ _____

35. $\left(\dfrac{-2a^2b^{-7}}{a^5b^{-4}}\right)^{-3}$ _____

Solve.

1-5

1. $y + 17 = 8$ _____   **2.** $m - 13 = 24$ _____   **3.** $x - 7 = -21$ _____

4. $7p = -63$ _____   **5.** $-8x = -96$ _____   **6.** $-\frac{4}{3}a = 16$ _____

7. $6t + 5 = 29$ _____   **8.** $-4x - 9 = -41$ _____   **9.** $12r - 5r = 42$ _____

10. $9a - 2 = 26 - 5a$ _____   **11.** $7m - 3 + 4m = m + 5 - 2m$

2-1

12. $\frac{2}{3}x + \frac{1}{9} = \frac{7}{9}$ _____   **13.** $1.1y - 0.4 = 1.8$ _____

14. $5(b + 4) = 35$ _____   **15.** $4n - (7n - 5) = -17$ _____

16. $(m + 5)(m + 6) = 0$ _____   **17.** $(3x + 7)(2x - 4) = 0$ _____

2-3

18. $V = abc$, for c _____   **19.** $2A = (a + b)h$, for h _____

20. $Q = \frac{1}{2}(a + b + c)W$, for W _____   **21.** $P = 2l + 2w$, for w _____

22. $\frac{1}{2}P = l + w$, for l _____   **23.** $y = -6 + 2x^2$, for x^2 _____

Evaluate each expression.

1-3

24. $-y$ for $y = -\frac{3}{4}$ _____   **25.** $2c - 4e$ for $c = 3$, and $e = 5$ _____

26. $6z - 2w$ for $z = 4$ and $w = -1$ _____   **27.** $|z| + z$ for $z = 4$ _____

28. $|w| + w$ for $w = -111$ _____   **29.** $\frac{4}{5}y + x$ for $y = -\frac{5}{4}$ and $x = 1$ _____

Perform the indicated operation and simplify.

1-1

30. $4 + (-7)$ _____   **31.** $\left(\frac{3}{4}\right)\left(\frac{7}{9}\right)\left(\frac{4}{7}\right)$ _____   **32.** $\frac{2}{5} \div \left(-\frac{8}{3}\right)$ _____

33. $-6.3 + 2.7$ _____   **34.** $-5 - (-13)$ _____   **35.** $-6 + (-10)$ _____

1-2

36. $(-5)(-13)$ _____   **37.** $|-6 + 2|$ _____   **38.** $-196 \div 14$ _____

39. $\left|\frac{2}{3}\right|$ _____   **40.** $(-2)(13)(14)(0)$ _____   **41.** $-\frac{3}{7} - \left(-\frac{4}{5}\right)$ _____

Solve. Then graph.

2-4

42. $x + 7 > 2$ _____   **43.** $y + 2 > 9$ _____   **44.** $t - 4 < -7$ _____

45. $2x \leq 14$ _____   **46.** $-2x \geq -14$ _____   **47.** $3y + 4 < 13$ _____

Solve. Then graph.

2-6

1. $5 < x + 3 < 10$ _____

2. $-3 \le 4x + 5 \le 9$ _____

3. $-3 \ge 7y - 3 \ge -24$ _____

4. $8 > \frac{1}{4}x + 6 > 7$ _____

5. $x + 2 < -1$ or $x + 2 > 1$ _____

6. $3x + 2 < -7$ or $x - 4 > -1$ _____

2-7

7. $|x| = 1$ _____

8. $|x| < 4$ _____

9. $|2x| \ge 6$ _____

10. $|3x + 2| \le 10$ _____

11. $|4x - 4| > 16$ _____

12. $\left|\frac{1}{2}x - 1\right| < 1$ _____

Solve.

2-5

13. A football team has won 4 out of 7 games played. If there are 16 games in a season, how many more games must be won to give the team, a season record of at least 60% games won out of all games played? _____

Simplify.

1-4

14. $5(3x - 2y)$ _____

15. $\frac{1}{2}a(4b - c)$ _____

16. $3a - 2(2a - b)$ _____

17. $-4(-m + 4) - 3(m + 2)$ _____

18. $c - 20c + 3(3 - 2c)$ _____

19. $x - [6 - 2(3x - 3)]$ _____

1-8

20. $11^{-4} \cdot 11^{-6} \cdot 11^7$ _____

21. $(3x^4y^{-3})(x^{11}y^7)$ _____

22. $(-3w^{-14}z^4)(-3w^8z^{-1})$ _____

23. $\frac{x^6}{x^7}$ _____

24. $\frac{-56a^{13}b^{-3}}{-8a^{12}b^{-4}}$ _____

25. $\frac{4^7q^{-10}r^{12}}{4^{-5}q^{-4}r^2}$ _____

26. $(7^{-2})^{-4}$ _____

27. $(13c^2d^{-4})^3$ _____

28. $(14^4x^{-2}y)^{-2}$ _____

29. $\left(\frac{2a^3b^{-3}}{5b^6}\right)^5$ _____

Multiply or divide and write the answer in scientific notation.

1-9

30. $\frac{4.2 \times 10^{-3}}{16.8 \times 10^{-12}}$ _____

31. $(7.67 \times 10^7)(3.82 \times 10^4)$ _____

32. $\frac{9.11 \times 10^4}{3.23 \times 10^7}$ _____

33. $(2.4 \times 10^{-10})(5.62 \times 10^{-4})$ _____

Graph each of the following.

3-2

1. $y = 5x + 4$ **2.** $y = -\dfrac{1}{2}x - 2$ **3.** $2x + 3y = 12$

3-4

4. $2x - 14 = 0$ **5.** $\dfrac{2}{3}y + 4 = 0$ **6.** $4a - 5b = 20$

3-3

7. $6r - 5s = 30$ **8.** $3y - 4x = 24$ **9.** $2y = -4 + 6x$

For each function, find the indicated function values.

3-3

10. $f(x) = 2x - 3$

    a. $f(-4)$ _____ **b.** $f(0)$ _____ **c.** $f\left(\dfrac{1}{2}\right)$ _____ **d.** $f(4)$ _____

11. $g(x) = 6x^2 - x - 2$

    a. $g(5)$ _____ **b.** $g\left(-\dfrac{1}{2}\right)$ _____ **c.** $g(0)$ _____ **d.** $g\left(\dfrac{2}{3}\right)$ _____

List the domain and the range for each of the following relations.

3-1

12. $\{(-3, -2), (0, -2), (1, 1), (2, 0)\}$ _____

13. $\{(-1, -4), (1, 0), (0, 2), (1, 3)\}$ _____

14. $\{(3, 3), (-1, -1), (0, 0), (1, -1), (3, -3)\}$ _____

3-2

15–17. Graph the relations in Exercises 12–14 above.

Which relations in Exercises 12–14 are functions?

3-3

18. _____ **19.** _____ **20.** _____

Simplify, leaving as little as possible inside absolute value signs.

2-7

21. $|5x|$ _____ **22.** $|y^3|$ _____ **23.** $|-16n|$ _____ **24.** $|a^8 b^9|$ _____

Solve.

2-2

25. Money is borrowed at 8% simple interest. After 1 year $594.00 pays off the loan. How much was borrowed originally?

_____

26. A stereo store drops the price of its top-of-the-line stereo system from $3300.000 to $2673.00 By what percent is the system discounted?

_____

Convert to decimal notation.

1-9

27. 5×10^{-6} _____ **28.** 5.43×10^{10} _____

29. 13.5×10^{-9} _____ **30.** $(6.002 \times 10^{-5})(1.4 \times 10^3)$ _____

Find the slope, if it exists, of each line.

3-5

1. $x = 7$ _____   **2.** $13 = -7y$ _____

3. $y = -9$ _____   **4.** $6x + 5 = 2x - 9$ _____

Find the slope and the y-intercept of each line.

3-6

5. $y = 5x - 4$ _____   **6.** $2y + 4x = 6$ _____

7. $3x = y + 7$ _____   **8.** $3x + 4y = 2$ _____

Find the equation of the line containing the given points with the indicated slope.

3-5

9. $(-4, -4); m = 0$ _____   **10.** $(3, 7); m = 2$ _____

11. $(0, 6); m = \dfrac{1}{2}$ _____   **12.** $(3, -3); m = -\dfrac{4}{3}$ _____

Find an equation of the line containing the following pairs of points.

3-6

13. $(2, 14)$ and $(-1, -1)$ _____   **14.** $(4, -4)$ and $(-4, 0)$ _____

15. $(3, 7)$ and $(7, 7)$ _____   **16.** $(5, -3)$ and $(15, 3)$ _____

Write an equation of the line containing the given point and parallel to the given line.

3-7

17. $(-2, 2), y = 3x + 4$ _____   **18.** $(4, -1), 2y = x + 6$ _____

19. $(-6, 3), 2y + 4x = 3$ _____   **20.** $(-9, -10), 3y + 5x = 4$ _____

Simplify.

1-4

21. $2(x - 2) - 3(2x - 4)$ _____   **22.** $2(3x + 4) - 4(2x - 5)$ _____

1-8

23. $(-a^2b^{-3})(-2a^{-2}b)$ _____   **24.** $(-2xy)(-2xy)(-2xy)$ _____

25. $\dfrac{a^4b^2c}{a^2b^{-1}c^4}$ _____   **26.** $\left(\dfrac{x^3y^5z^{-2}}{x^7y^2z^{-7}}\right)^3$ _____

Graph each of the following.

3-9

27. $f(x) = |2x - 1|$ **28.** $f(x) = |2x| - 1$ **29.** $f(x) = 3|x| + 4$

Solve.

2-1

30. $2x + 4 = 16$ _____   **31.** $y - 3 = 2y + 14$ _____

32. $3(y + 2) = 2(y - 8)$ _____   **33.** $y - 2(y - 2) = 6$ _____

34. $(a - 3)(2a + 4) = 0$ _____   **35.** $(3x - 4)(5x + 1) = 0$ _____

3-9   Suppose $f(x) = \frac{1}{2}x + 2$, $g(x) = 3x - 5$, $h(x) = 2x^2 + 1$. Find the following.

1. $f(g(1))$ _____   2. $f(h(-2))$ _____   3. $h(g(-1))$ _____

4. $g(f(-4))$ _____   5. $h(f(-5))$ _____   6. $f(h(-5))$ _____

7. $g(g(x))$ _____   8. $g(h(x))$ _____

3-7   Write an equation of the line containing the given point and perpendicular to the given line.

9. $(4, -3)$, $y - 2x = -6$ _____   10. $(0, 2)$, $y + 4x = 11$ _____

11. $(-3, 1)$, $y + 3x = -8$ _____   12. $(-7, -1)$, $2y - 3x = 3$ _____

3-5   Find the slope of the line containing each pair of points.

13. $(7, 8)$ and $(4, 12)$ _____   14. $(2, 13)$ and $(6, 3)$ _____

3-4   Tell which of the following equations are linear.

15. $x^2 - y = 4$ _____   16. $3x - 4y = 6$ _____   17. $x + \dfrac{x}{y} = 7$ _____

4-1   Solve graphically.

18. $y = 2x - 6$
    $-2y = x + 2$

19. $y = 5x - 13$
    $5x + y = 17$

20. $6y + 4x = 22$
    $y = \dfrac{3}{2}x + \dfrac{3}{2}$

Use linear combinations or the substitution method to solve these systems.

4-2   21. $y = 2x$
        $3y + x = 14$ _____

22. $y = 3x + 1$
    $y - 5x = 1$ _____

23. $y = 2x - 4$
    $x = 5y - 7$ _____

24. $2y + 5x = 14$
    $-2y + 3x = 2$ _____

25. $3x - 6y = 12$
    $2x + 3y = 1$ _____

26. $2x + 3y = 15$
    $3x - 7y = -12$ _____

27. $2x + 4y = 10$
    $x + 2y = 5$ _____

28. $2x + 3y = 7$
    $-4x - 6y = 4$ _____

29. $5x - 2y = 29$
    $7x + 5y = 25$ _____

4-4   30. $x + y + z = 7$
        $-x + 3y + 3z = 13$
        $2x + 2y - z = 2$ _____

31. $2x + y + z = 4$
    $-2x - 2y + 2z = -2$
    $x - 3y - 2z = 9$ _____

32. $3x + 4y - 2z = 10$
    $2x + 5y + 3z = 20$
    $7x + 3y + z = 22$ _____

33. $2x + 5y - 3z = -3$
    $6x - 8y + 2z = 4$
    $5x + 4y - 3z = -4$ _____

Solve.

4-3

1. A chemistry student needs 10 L of a 12% acid solution. The laboratory has ample amounts of 10% and 20% acid solutions. How many liters of each solution should the student mix?

_____

2. A chemistry student needs 15 L of a 32% acid solution. The laboratory has ample amounts of 30% and 40% acid solutions. How many liters of each solution should the student mix?

_____

3. In triangle ABC, the measure of angle C is 18° greater than three times the measure of angle A. The measure of angle B is 5 times the measure of angle A. Find the angle measures.

_____

4. The sum of three numbers is 270. The second plus twice the first is 36 more than the third. The first plus the third is 27 less than twice the second. Find the numbers.

_____

3-8

5. The Apollo missions used the Saturn V rocket. The velocity at the end of the first stage was approximately 6375 m/h, $2\frac{1}{2}$ minutes after launch. At the end of the second stage, 9 minutes after launch, the rocket's velocity was 15,150 m/h.
  a. Fit a linear function to the data points.
  b. Use the function to predict the velocity 10 minutes after launch.
  c. Predict the velocity at the end of the third stage, 15 minutes after launch.

_____

_____

_____

Graph. Find the coordinates of any vertices formed.

4-7

6. $x \geq 0$
$2y + x < 6$
$y > x - 3$ _____

7. $y < 0$
$2y \leq 3x + 6$
$10y \geq 3x - 18$ _____

8. $2y + 5x < 23$
$4y < 3x + 7$
$3y + x \geq 2$ _____

Determine whether the graphs of each pair of equations are parallel, perpendicular, or neither.

3-7

9. $y = \frac{3}{4}x - 7$
$3y = -4x + 8$ _____

10. $y = 4x - 10$
$2y - 8x = 5$ _____

11. $y = 3x - 5$
$5y = 3x + 1$ _____

12. $4y + 3x = 12$
$3y - 4x = 9$ _____

13. $y = 2x + 6$
$3y = 6x + 18$ _____

14. $5y = 2x + 11$
$2y + 5x = 5$ _____

Determine whether the systems in Examples 9–14 are consistent or inconsistent.

4-6

15. _____ **16.** _____ **17.** _____ **18.** _____ **19.** _____ **20.** _____

Determine whether the systems in Examples 9–14 are dependent.

4-6

21. _____ **22.** _____ **23.** _____ **24.** _____ **25.** _____ **26.** _____

Simplify.

1-4

1. $3a - 7a - 11b - 13b$ _____

2. $2x - [6 - 4(2x - 3)]$ _____

3. $4\{-13 + 2[8 - 3(4 - 2)]\}$ _____

4. $6b - 2[-9 - 6(5b - 4)]$ _____

1-8

5. $3[(2 + 3 \cdot 2^2) - 16 \div 4 \cdot 2]$ _____

6. $[2(7 - 4)^2 - 7] \cdot (4 - 2 \cdot 5)$ _____

7. $2[(6 + 4 \cdot 3^2) \div 7 \cdot 3]$ _____

8. $2[(6 \div 3 \cdot 4 \div 2 - 3 \cdot 2)^2 - 3^2]$ _____

Add or subtract.

5-2

9. $(4x^3 - 2x^2 + 5x - 3) - (7x^3 + 2x^2 - 3x - 5)$ _____

10. $(3a^2 - 4ab + b^2 - 8) - (-4a^2 - ab + 5b^2 + 2)$ _____

11. $(x^4 - 3x^3 + 4x - 7) - (6x^4 + 4x^3 + 2x^2 - 3)$ _____

12. $(3x^4 - 5x^3 - 8x^2 - x) + (9x^3 + 2x^2 - 3x - 9)$ _____

13. $(6x^2 + 4xy - 3x + 6) - (7x^2 + 4xy - 9x - 4)$ _____

Multiply.

1-8

14. $(3x^2y^4)(2x^3y)$ _____

15. $(x^3y^2)^2(x^{-8}y)$ _____

16. $(5a^9b^6c)(2a^{-4}b^{-8}c^3)$ _____

17. $(3a^2b^{-4}c)^{-3}$ _____

5-3

18. $6a^2 - 2ab + 3b^2$ and $2a - b$ _____

19. $4x^2 + x - 5$ and $-x + 3$ _____

20. $(x + 7)(2x^2 - 4x - 6)$ _____

21. $(x - y)(x^2 + xy + y^2)$ _____

22. $(3a + 5b)(2a + 3b)$ _____

23. $(4x + 3)(3x - 2)$ _____

24. $(3s - 2t)^2$ _____

25. $(7x + 2y)^2$ _____

26. $(2x + 6)(2x - 6)$ _____

27. $(3a + 5b)(3a - 5b)$ _____

Factor.

5-4

28. $bx - by + bz$ _____

29. $12wx - 8wy + 16wz$ _____

30. $9y^2 - (x^2 + 6x + 9)$ _____

31. $25y^4 - y^2z^2$ _____

32. $x^4 - 64x^2$ _____

33. $x(y^2 - 5) - 3(y^2 - 5)$ _____

34. $12x^2 + 9x + 4x^3$ _____

35. $ab + ad + cb + cd$ _____

36. $27a^2 + 75 - 90a$ _____

37. $3a^4 - 48b^4$ _____

38. $2b^2 - 12bc + 18c^2 - 18d^2$ _____

39. $x^3 + 6x^2 + 4x + 24$ _____

Factor.

5-5

1. $x^2 + 3x - 10$ _____

2. $x^3 - 125y^3$ _____

3. $x^3 + 8x^2 + 15x$ _____

4. $8t^3 + 1000s^3$ _____

5. $x^2 - 11x + 24$ _____

6. $x^2 + 10x + 24$ _____

7. $x^2 - 10x - 24$ _____

8. $x^2 - 2x - 24$ _____

9. $3x^4 - 48y^4$ _____

10. $12x^2 - 13x - 4$ _____

5-7

11. $12x^2 - 77x + 30$ _____

12. $12x^2 - 25x + 12$ _____

13. $12x^2 + 40x + 25$ _____

14. $18x^2 + 39x + 20$ _____

15. $m^6 - n^6$ _____

16. $x^2 + 7x + 12$ _____

17. $x^2 - 13x + 12$ _____

18. $x^2 + 4x - 12$ _____

19. $5a + 5c - 12a - 12c$ _____

20. $ax - xb - ay + yb$ _____

21. $54w^3 - 128z^3$ _____

22. $81m^3 + 375n^3$ _____

23. $9c^2 - 6cd + d^2$ _____

24. $a^2 - 8a + 16 - b^2$ _____

25. $x^2 + 12x - y^2 + 36$ _____

26. $2x^3 + 6x^2 - 16x - 48$ _____

27. $w^2 - 10w - 9z^2 + 25$ _____

28. $m^5 + 2m^3 - 7m^2 - 14$ _____

Solve.

2-1

29. $4(x - 2) = x + 1$ _____

30. $5x - 13 = 3(x - 5)$ _____

2-4

31. $(3a - 4)(3a + 1) = 0$ _____

32. $-\frac{1}{3}y - \frac{1}{2}y > 10$ _____

2-7

33. $13 \leq 3y + 4 < 18$ _____

34. $|3x + 2| \geq 11$ _____

5-7

35. $y^2 = 225$ _____

36. $x^2 + 20x = 0$ _____

37. $x^2 - x = 12$ _____

38. $-14x + 3x^2 = 24$ _____

39. $x^2 = 4$ _____

40. $4x^2 - 4x = 3$ _____

41. $2x(x + 5) + 3x(x + 5) = 0$ _____

42. $2x(x + 5) + 3(x + 5) = 0$ _____

2-1

43. $2(x + 5) + 3(x + 5) = 0$ _____

44. $2(4x + 5) - 3(x - 4) = -13$ _____

Multiply and simplify.

1-8

1. $(4x^l y^m)(-3x^5 y^n)$ _____

2. $(-2a^3 b^{-2})^3(a^2 b^4)$ _____

3. $(3a - 5b)(4a + 2b)$ _____

4. $(2s^2 + 6t^2)(2s^2 - 6t^2)$ _____

6-1

5. $\dfrac{y^2 - 36}{y^2} \cdot \dfrac{y^2 - 3y}{y^2 - 4y - 12}$ _____

6. $\dfrac{x^2 + 8x + 16}{x^2 - 16} \cdot \dfrac{x + 6}{x + 4}$ _____

7. $\dfrac{a^2 - 9}{2a + 12} \cdot \dfrac{a + 6}{a - 3}$ _____

8. $\dfrac{m^2 - 4m - 21}{m^2 - m - 6} \cdot \dfrac{5m + 10}{5m + 15}$ _____

Divide and simplify.

1-8

9. $\left(\dfrac{2^{-7} a^4 b^4}{2^{-2} a^3 b^{-2}}\right)^3$ _____

10. $\dfrac{x^{5a} y^b z^{2c}}{x^{2a} y^4 z^{2c}}$ _____

6-1

11. $\dfrac{4x - 24}{x} \div \dfrac{x - 6}{x}$ _____

12. $\dfrac{y^2 - 16}{y} \div \dfrac{y + 4}{y + 3}$ _____

13. $\dfrac{36b^2 - 1}{b^2 - 36} \div \dfrac{6b - 1}{b - 6}$ _____

14. $\dfrac{4x^2 - 25}{x^2 - 16} \div \dfrac{2x - 5}{x + 4}$ _____

6-4

15. $(7y^4 - 21y^3 - 28y^2) \div 7y$ _____

16. $(x^2 y + x^4 y^4 - x^6 y^2) \div x^2 y$ _____

17. $(x^2 + 10x + 24) \div (x + 4)$ _____

18. $(y^2 - 2y - 15) \div (y - 5)$ _____

19. $(a^2 - 6a - 9) \div (a - 3)$ _____

20. $(y^2 - 49) \div (y + 7)$ _____

Perform the indicated operations. Simplify when possible.

5-2

21. $(8x^2 - 3xy + 2y^2 - 4) + (-7x^2 - 5xy + 6y^2 + 4)$ _____

22. $(9x^2 - 3x - 9) + (-x^2 + 3y + 7) + (-4x^2 + 2xy + 5)$ _____

23. $(2x^2 + 3xy - 6y^2 + 4) - (-x^2 + 3xy + 6y^2 + 9)$ _____

6-2

24. $\dfrac{s^2}{s - t} + \dfrac{t^2}{t - s}$ _____

25. $\dfrac{4}{y} - \dfrac{9}{-y}$ _____

26. $\dfrac{2x - 6}{x^2 - 9} - \dfrac{3 - x}{9 - x^2}$ _____

27. $\dfrac{x - 3}{x + 5} + \dfrac{x + 2}{x - 4}$ _____

28. $\dfrac{4ab}{a^2 - b^2} + \dfrac{a - b}{a + b}$ _____

29. $\dfrac{s}{s^2 - s - 12} + \dfrac{3}{s + 3}$ _____

Solve.

6-9

1. With pressure and volume constant, the number of moles (n) of a gas varies inversely as its temperature (T). The temperature of a certain gas is 400 K when it contains 5 moles. How many moles of the gas are there when the temperature drops to 300 K? _____

6-7

2. The new RGH-5 microprocessor executes instructions 200,000,000 words/s faster than the ZP-13. While the ZP-13 processes 8,000,000 words of data, the RGH-5 processes 10,000,000 words. Find the rate at which each processes data. _____

5-8

3. Kim is installing a skylight to conserve energy. She wants the width 50 cm less than the length and a total area of 15,000 cm². What are the dimensions? _____

Solve.

1-5

4. $3x - 7 = 4$ _____

5. $0.7(5x + 10) = 14 - \frac{1}{3}(6x - 12)$ _____

5-7

6. $x^2 - 8x + 7 = 0$ _____

7. $36z^2 = 121$ _____

2-1

8. $2x(x - 3) = 5(3 - x)$ _____

9. $m(m - 6)(2m + 3) = 0$ _____

6-6

10. $\dfrac{3}{y - 2} = \dfrac{6}{y + 3}$ _____

11. $\dfrac{30}{x + 7} - \dfrac{32}{x} = -\dfrac{16}{x}$ _____

12. $\dfrac{5}{y - 3} + \dfrac{3y - 5}{y^2 - 9} = \dfrac{6}{y + 3}$ _____

13. $\dfrac{3}{x - 2} = \dfrac{x}{x^2 + 3x - 10} - \dfrac{2}{x + 5}$ _____

Solve each formula for the given letter.

2-3

14. $E = \dfrac{hc}{\lambda}$; h _____

15. $V = \dfrac{1}{5}lw(a + b)$; b _____

16. $k = \dfrac{1}{2}I\omega^2$; ω^2 _____

17. $E = \dfrac{3}{2}kT$; T _____

18. $E = \dfrac{1}{2}mv^2$; v^2 _____

19. $g = \dfrac{GM}{R^2}$; M _____

6-8

20. $m^2 = \dfrac{m_0^2 c^2}{c^2 - v^2}$; c^2 _____

21. $M = \dfrac{pq}{r + ps}$; p _____

22. $\dfrac{1}{\ell_1} + \dfrac{1}{\ell_2} = \dfrac{1}{L}$; L _____

23. $m(x_2 - x_1) + y_1 = y_2$; m _____

24. $kv = \dfrac{m + M}{m}$; m _____

25. $Q = \dfrac{rs}{s + t}$; s _____

Simplify.

7-1

1. $\sqrt{36z^2}$ _____

2. $\sqrt{(-3a)^2}$ _____

3. $\sqrt[3]{-125x^3}$ _____

4. $\sqrt[3]{8x^3}$ _____

5. $\sqrt[3]{54l^5m^4n^3}$ _____

6. $\sqrt[4]{20x^9y^7z^5}$ _____

7-3

7. $\sqrt{\dfrac{25}{36}}$ _____

8. $\sqrt{\dfrac{121}{x^2}}$ _____

9. $\sqrt[3]{\dfrac{125x^7}{27y^6}}$ _____

7-5

10. $\sqrt{(20c^2d)^3}$ _____

11. $(\sqrt[3]{10x^7y})^7$ _____

12. $(\sqrt[3]{49u^3b^7})^7$ _____

Write the radical expressions in Exercises 10–12 with rational exponents.

7-5

13. _____

14. _____

15. _____

Multiply and simplify by factoring.

7-2

16. $\sqrt{3}\sqrt{13}$ _____

17. $\sqrt[3]{10x}\sqrt[3]{5xy}$ _____

18. $\sqrt[6]{x-y}\sqrt[6]{(x-y)^4}$ _____

19. $\sqrt{8}\sqrt{36}$ _____

20. $\sqrt{3c^5}\sqrt{12d^3}$ _____

21. $\sqrt[3]{4x^2y}\sqrt[3]{x^5y^3}$ _____

7-4

22. $(\sqrt{2}+\sqrt{b})^2$ _____

23. $(\sqrt{x}+\sqrt{y})(\sqrt{x}+\sqrt{2})$ _____

24. $\sqrt[3]{3}(\sqrt[3]{9}+\sqrt[3]{18a})$ _____

25. $(\sqrt{12}+3\sqrt{5})(2\sqrt{3}+2\sqrt{7})$ _____

Rationalize the denominator.

7-4

26. $\sqrt{\dfrac{3}{7}}$ _____

27. $\dfrac{2\sqrt{5}}{4\sqrt{6}}$ _____

28. $\sqrt[3]{\dfrac{9}{4}}$ _____

29. $\dfrac{\sqrt[3]{4a^3}}{\sqrt[3]{5b^2}}$ _____

30. $\dfrac{4\sqrt{7}-\sqrt{10}}{\sqrt{5}-3\sqrt{3}}$ _____

Use synthetic division to find the quotient and remainder.

6-5

31. $(x^3+4x^2-x-4)\div(x+1)$ _____

32. $(2x^3-4x^2+3x+1)\div(x+2)$ _____

33. $(x^3+2x^2-6x+3)\div(x-3)$ _____

Divide.

6-1

34. $\dfrac{5a-20}{a^2-7a+12}\div\dfrac{a+3}{a^2-9}$ _____

6-4

35. $(16x^6+28x^4-32x^2)\div 4x^2$ _____

36. $(y^3-3y^2+4y-5)\div(y-2)$ _____

Add or subtract.

7-7

1. $-3i + (5 + 4i)$ _____

2. $(3 - 4i) + (7 + 6i)$ _____

3. $(2 + 5i) - (9 - 4i)$ _____

4. $8i - (-3 + 9i)$ _____

5. $(11 - 6i) + (4 + 2i)$ _____

6. $(4 + i) - (-7 + i)$ _____

7. $3\sqrt[3]{2} - 5\sqrt[3]{2} + 4\sqrt[3]{2}$ _____

8. $6\sqrt{63} - 2\sqrt{28} + 5\sqrt{7}$ _____

9. $4\sqrt{3x^3} + \sqrt{12x} - \sqrt{27x^3}$ _____

10. $\sqrt[3]{24x^4y} - 9\sqrt[3]{3xy}$ _____

11. $\sqrt{12y - 4} + \sqrt{27y - 9}$ _____

12. $\sqrt{x^3 + 3x^2} - \sqrt{16x + 48}$ _____

Multiply.

7-7

13. $\sqrt{-6} \cdot 3i$ _____

14. $\sqrt{-5} \cdot \sqrt{-15}$ _____

15. $-\sqrt{-4} \cdot \sqrt{-12}$ _____

7-9

16. $2i \cdot 3i$ _____

17. $(5i)^2$ _____

18. $(3 - 4i)(5 + 6i)$ _____

19. $(3 - 4i)^2$ _____

20. $(2 + 7i)(5 - 4i)$ _____

21. $(8 - i)(8 + i)$ _____

5-3

22. $(3 + 4b)^2$ _____

23. $(2x + 7y)(5x - 4y)$ _____

24. $(3a + 4b)(3a - 4b)$ _____

25. $(2a + 7b)(2a - 7b)$ _____

26. $(2 - 3w)(2 + 3w)$ _____

27. $(5x + y)(x + 6y)$ _____

Divide.

7-9

28. $\dfrac{2 + 3i}{2 - 3i}$ _____

29. $\dfrac{i}{1 + i}$ _____

30. $\dfrac{\sqrt{3} + 3i}{\sqrt{3} - 3i}$ _____

6-4

31. $(9a - 16b^2) \div (3a + 4b)$ _____

32. $(16b^2 + 24b + 9) \div (4b + 3)$ _____

33. $(6x^3 - 11x^2 + 11x - 1) \div (2x - 3)$ _____

Solve.

7-6

34. $\sqrt{4x + 1} = 3$ _____

35. $\sqrt[3]{9x + 1} = 4$ _____

36. $\sqrt[4]{5x - 4} = 2$ _____

37. $\sqrt{x + 5} = \sqrt{2x + 2}$ _____

38. $\sqrt{3x - 4} = 2\sqrt{x + 1}$ _____

39. $\sqrt{x + 3} + \sqrt{5x + 4} = 5$ _____

40. $\sqrt{4x + 9} - \sqrt{x + 6} = -1$ _____

41. $\sqrt{2x + 6} = \sqrt{4x + 5} - 1$ _____

7-10

42. $(2 + 2i)x - i = 3i$ _____

43. $3ix + 3 - 3i = (2 + 5i)x - i$ _____

44. $(1 - i)x + 3 - 4i = 5 + 5x$ _____

45. $(3 - 2i)x + 3 = (4 + 3i)x - 4i$ _____

MIXED REVIEW 15

For use after Lesson 8-4

NAME _____

DATE _____

Solve.

1-5

1. $z + \dfrac{3}{4} = \dfrac{2}{3}$ _____

2. $\dfrac{3}{4}z = \dfrac{2}{3}$ _____

3. $3z - 4 = \dfrac{2}{3}$ _____

2-1

4. $3z - 4 = 3z + 2$ _____

5. $2(w + 5) = 2w + 10$ _____

6. $3(w + 7) = 4(w + 7)$ _____

7. $(a - 6)(2a + 9) = 0$ _____

8. $3(a + 4) = 24$ _____

9. $(5x + 3)(3x + 7) = 0$ _____

8-1

10. $8y^2 + 29y - 12 = 0$ _____

11. $y^2 - 5y - 36 = 0$ _____

12. $y^2 + 2y - 24 = 0$ _____

13. $15y^2 - 11y + 2 = 0$ _____

14. $2y^2 - 5y - 7 = 0$ _____

15. $2y^2 + 3y - 27 = 0$ _____

16. $4x^2 = 9$ _____

17. $13x^2 = 0$ _____

18. $2a^2 - 5 = 0$ _____

19. $x^2 + 16 = 0$ _____

20. $9x^2 + 25 = 0$ _____

21. $3x^2 + 7 = 0$ _____

22. $2x^2 - 5x = 0$ _____

23. $9x^2 - 4x = 0$ _____

24. $x^2 - 7x = 0$ _____

5-7

25. $a^2 + 6a + 2 = 0$ _____

26. $a^2 + 6a - 2 = 0$ _____

27. $2x^2 + 4x - 3 = 0$ _____

28. $2x^2 + 4x + 3 = 0$ _____

29. $2x^2 - 4x = 3$ _____

30. $-2x^2 + 4x = 3$ _____

8-3

31. $4 + \dfrac{8}{c} + \dfrac{1}{c^2} = 0$ _____

32. $4c^2 + 8c = 1$ _____

33. $2x + x(x - 5) = 0$ _____

34. $(3z - 1)^2 + 15z = 5$ _____

Solve by completing the square.

8-1

35. $x^2 + 4x - 2 = 0$ _____

36. $x^2 - 6y + 1 = 0$ _____

37. $2y^2 - 5y + 4 = 0$ _____

38. $3x^2 + 7x - 9 = 0$ _____

Find an equation having the specified numbers as solutions.

7-10

39. $6i, -6i$ _____

40. $3 + i, 3 - i$ _____

41. $\sqrt{2} + i, \sqrt{2} - i$ _____

42. $2 + 2i, 2 - 2i$ _____

8-4

43. $6, -6$ _____

44. $4, 2$ _____

45. $\sqrt{2}, -\sqrt{2}$ _____

46. $2\pi, -5\pi$ _____

Solve each formula for the given letter.

6-8

1. $A = P + Prt; P$ _____

2. $m = \dfrac{y_2 - y_1}{x_2 - x_1}, x_2$ _____

3. $y = mx + b; m$ _____

4. $I = Prt; r$ _____

2-3

5. $V = \pi r^2 h; r^2$ _____

6. $x^2 + y^2 = r^2; x^2$ _____

8-6

7. $a^2 + b^2 + c^2 = t^2; c$ _____

8. $F = \dfrac{mv^2}{r}; v$ _____

9. $r = \sqrt{\dfrac{GMm}{F}}; M$ _____

10. $A = \dfrac{1}{4}\pi r^2; r$ _____

11. $P = \dfrac{E^2}{R}; E$ _____

12. $2 = \omega t + \alpha t^2; t$ _____

Solve.

8-5

13. $10x - \sqrt{x} - 3 = 0$ _____

14. $2x^4 - 9x^2 + 9 = 0$ _____

15. $5w^{\frac{1}{2}} - 7w^{\frac{1}{4}} + 2 = 0$ _____

16. $2\sqrt[3]{x^2} - \sqrt[3]{x} = 6$ _____

5-7

17. $12x^2 - 16x + 5 = 0$ _____

18. $y^2 - 13y + 12 = 0$ _____

19. $25x^2 - 36 = 0$ _____

20. $-16y^2 + 49 = 0$ _____

8-1

21. $(w + 2)(w + 7) = 6$ _____

22. $-6(m + 7) = m(m + 7)$ _____

Determine the nature of the solutions of each equation.

8-9

23. $x^2 + 5x - 10 = 0$ _____

24. $x^2 + 5x + 10 = 0$ _____

25. $m^2 + 7 = 0$ _____

26. $y^2 - 8 = 0$ _____

27. $z^2 - 8z + 16 = 0$ _____

28. $8n^2 + 5n + \dfrac{3}{4} = 0$ _____

Find an equation of variation where

6-9

29. y varies inversely as x, and $y = 0.3$ when $x = 0.6$. _____

8-7

30. y varies directly as the square of x, and $y = 0.12$ when $x = 0.2$. _____

31. y varies inversely as the square of x, and $y = 3$ when $x = 2$. _____

32. y varies jointly as x and z, and $y = 42$ when $x = 7$ and $z = 3$. _____

33. y varies directly as x and inversely as z, and $y = 3$ when $x = 9$ and $z = 12$. _____

34. y varies jointly as x and z and inversely as w, and $y = \dfrac{5}{3}$ when $x = 5$, $z = 6$, and $w = 18$.

Test for symmetry with respect to the *x*-axis, the *y*-axis, and the origin.

9-1

1. $4y^2 = 3x^2 - 6$ _____

2. $5x - 3 = 2y$ _____

3. $3y = 2x^3$ _____

4. $y^3 = 4x^2$ _____

5. $6y^2 = 3x^2 + 11$ _____

6. $4x^3 = 3y^3 + 8$ _____

7. $3y^2 = -6x^2 + 2$ _____

8. $9x = -9y$ _____

9. $5y = 8$ _____

10. $3y = 5x^2 - 4x$ _____

11. $9x = |y|$ _____

12. $3x - 3y = 0$ _____

Solve.

8-6, 8-7

13. Two houseflies, Sam and Elise, take off from the picnic table at the same time heading south and east, respectively. Sam, after eating more than he should, travels 50 cm/s slower than Elise. After 10 seconds they are 25.00 m (2500 cm) apart. Find the speed of Sam and Elise.

_____

14. The pressure (*P*) of a gas varies jointly as the number of moles (*n*) and the temperature (*T*), and inversely as the volume (*V*). One mole at 1000 K in a volume of 10 L has a pressure of 8.23 atm. What is the pressure of one mole of gas at 500 K in a volume of 10 L?

_____

What is the pressure of two moles of gas at 300 K in a volume of 1 L?

_____

Here is a graph of $y = f(x)$. Sketch these graphs.

9-2

15. $y = f(x) + 2$

16. $y = f(x) - 4$

17. $y = f(x) + 3$

18. $y = f(x + 2)$

19. $y = f(x - 3)$

20. $y = f(x - 1)$

9-3

21. $y = 2f(x)$

22. $y = \frac{1}{2}f(x)$

23. $y = -2f(x)$

24. $y = f(2x)$

25. $y = f\left(\frac{1}{2}x\right)$

26. $y = f(-3x)$

Find the sum and the product of the solutions.

8-4

27. $2x^2 - 3x + 4 = 0$ _____

28. $x^2 + 4x - 1 = 0$ _____

29. $y^2 = 81$ _____

Find a quadratic equation for which the sum and the product of the solutions are as given.

8-4

30. Sum $= -6$; product $= \pi$ _____

31. Sum $= \sqrt{2}$; product $= -\frac{1}{8}$ _____

Use a calculator or a square root table to approximate solutions to the nearest tenth.

8-3

32. $4x^2 + 2x - 3 = 0$ _____

33. $-2x^2 - 3x + 4 = 0$ _____

34. $3x^2 + 5x - 2 = 0$ _____

35. $2x^2 - 6x + 7 = 0$ _____

36. $3x^2 + 7x - 2 = 0$ _____

37. $5x^2 - 3x - 4 = 0$ _____

MIXED REVIEW 18

For use after Lesson 9-8

NAME _____

DATE _____

Use the properties of exponents to simplify.

7-5

1. $3^{\frac{1}{4}}3^{\frac{2}{3}}$ _____

2. $6^{\frac{3}{5}}6^{\frac{4}{7}}$ _____

3. $(7^{\frac{2}{3}})^{\frac{4}{5}}$ _____

4. $(2.4^{\frac{1}{2}})^{\frac{3}{7}}$ _____

5. $\dfrac{5^{\frac{7}{8}}}{5^{\frac{3}{4}}}$ _____

6. $\dfrac{9^{\frac{2}{5}}}{9^{\frac{5}{6}}}$ _____

Write as a single radical expression.

7-5

7. $(a^3b^2)^{\frac{1}{5}}$ _____

8. $x^{\frac{2}{7}}$ _____

9. $y^{\frac{6}{5}}$ _____

10. $(c^2d^6)^{\frac{1}{7}}$ _____

11. $p^{\frac{1}{3}} \cdot q^{\frac{1}{9}} \cdot r^{\frac{1}{6}}$ _____

12. $\sqrt{y}\sqrt[3]{y+3}$ _____

13. $\dfrac{m^{\frac{10}{21}} \cdot n^{\frac{2}{7}}}{m^{\frac{5}{21}} \cdot n^{-\frac{3}{7}}}$ _____

Find the linear function that fits each pair of data points.

3-8

14. $(0, 6), (2, 6)$ _____

15. $(-5, 6), (-3, -2)$ _____

Find the quadratic function that fits each set of data points.

9-8

16. $(0, 6), (1, 3), (2, 6)$ _____

17. $(-5, 6), (-3, -2), (-2, 0)$ _____

Find the equation of the line, in slope-intercept form, containing the following pairs of points.

3-6

18. $(-3, 1), (6, 4)$ _____

19. $(-1, -5), (1, -1)$ _____

20. $(-4, 1), (4, -5)$ _____

21. $(2, 2), (4, -3)$ _____

Graph the function and find the vertex, the line of symmetry, and the minimum or maximum value for each of the following.

9-4

22. $f(x) = -(x + 4)^2$ _____

23. $f(x) = 2(x - 4)^2$ _____

9-5

24. $f(x) = 4(x - 3)^2 + 1$ _____

25. $f(x) = -2(x + 4)^2 - 3$ _____

For each function find the standard form, the vertex, the line of symmetry, and the minimum or maximum value.

9-5

26. $f(x) = 11(x - 9)^2 + 17$ _____

27. $f(x) = -3\pi(x + 24.4)^2 - \sqrt{23}$ _____

9-6

28. $f(x) = -x^2 - 6x - 13$ _____

29. $f(x) = 3x^2 - 6x + 29$ _____

Find the distance between the points.

10-1

1. $(-12, 0)$ and $(-47, 0)$ _____

2. $(-6, 0)$ and $(22, 0)$ _____

3. $(-1, -4)$ and $(4, 8)$ _____

4. $(-2, 1)$ and $(4, -7)$ _____

5. $(1, 1)$ and $(4, -5)$ _____

6. $(-3, 5)$ and $(5, 1)$ _____

Find the center and the radius of each circle. Then graph the circle.

10-2

7. $x^2 + y^2 + 10x - 2y + 1 = 0$ _____

8. $x^2 + y^2 - 4x + 6y + 8 = 0$ _____

For each ellipse find the center, the vertices, and the foci, and draw a graph.

10-3

9. $\dfrac{x^2}{16} + \dfrac{y^2}{4} = 1$ _____

10. $3x^2 + 4y^2 = 12$ _____

11. $\dfrac{(x-1)^2}{25} + \dfrac{(y-3)^2}{9} = 1$ _____

12. $4(x+4)^2 + 2(y+2)^2 = 64$ _____

13. $4x^2 + 9y^2 - 24x + 36y + 36 = 0$ _____

For each hyperbola find the center, the vertices, the foci, and the asymptotes. Then draw a graph.

10-4

14. $9y^2 - x^2 = 9$ _____

15. $\dfrac{(x-5)^2}{4} - \dfrac{(y+7)^2}{9} = 1$ _____

16. $4x^2 - y^2 + 16x + 2y + 11 = 0$ _____

17. $4y^2 - 9x^2 + 18x - 40y + 55 = 0$ _____

Find the x-intercepts.

9-7

18. $f(x) = 3x^2 - 6x - 4$ _____

19. $f(x) = x^2 + 3x + 2$ _____

20. $f(x) = 3x^2 - 6x + 4$ _____

21. $f(x) = -2x^2 + 5x - 1$ _____

22. $f(x) = 4x^2 - 12x + 9$ _____

23. $f(x) = -3x^2 + 9x - 7$ _____

Use synthetic division to find the quotient and the remainder.

6-5

24. $(x^2 - 2x + 5) \div (x - 2)$ _____

25. $(3x^3 + 7x^2 - 2x + 12) \div (x + 3)$ _____

26. $(x^4 - 12x^2 + 3) \div (x + 4)$ _____

For each parabola find the vertex, the focus, and the directrix. Then draw a graph.

10-5

1. $y^2 = 8x$ _____

2. $x^2 = -4y$ _____

3. $(y - 2)^2 - 2(x + 3)$ _____

4. $x^2 + 2y + 2x - 7 = 0$ _____

5. $x^2 + y - 6x + 10 = 0$ _____

6. $y^2 - 4x + 4y - 20 = 0$ _____

Solve each system graphically. Then solve algebraically.

10-6

7. $x^2 + y^2 = 25$
   $2y + 5 = x$ _____

8. $2x^2 + 9y^2 = 18$
   $y = x + 3$ _____

9. $x^2 = 5 - y$
   $y = x + 3$ _____

10. $x^2 + y^2 = 25$
   $y^2 - x^2 = 7$ _____

10-7

11. $x^2 + 4y^2 = 32$
   $x^2 - 2y^2 = 8$ _____

12. $x^2 + y^2 = 25$
   $xy = 12$ _____

13. $9x^2 + y^2 = 9$
   $9y^2 - 16x^2 = 144$ _____

14. $x^2 + y^2 = 16$
   $64x^2 + 25y^2 = 1600$ _____

Solve.

4-2

15. $3y = 2x + 5$
   $y = 2x - 1$ _____

16. $2y + 5x = 23$
   $5y - 2x = -15$ _____

17. $y + 14 = -4x$
   $2y + 13 = -3x$ _____

18. $3y = x + 12$
   $y + 3x = -6$ _____

4-4

19. $x + y + z = 6$
   $2x - y + 3z = 7$
   $3x - y + z = 8$ _____

20. $2x + 2y - z = -3$
   $3x + 4y + z = -8$
   $-7x - 5y + z = 11$ _____

4-1

21–24. Solve the systems in Exercises 15–18 graphically.

Find the standard form and the slope of each equation in Exercises 15–18.

3-6

25. a. _____

26. a. _____

b. _____

b. _____

27. a. _____

28. a. _____

b. _____

b. _____

Determine whether the graphs of each pair of equations in Exercises 15–18 are perpendicular.

3-7

29. _____

30. _____

31. _____

32. _____

Divide each $P(x)$ by $D(x)$. Then express the dividend as $P(x) = D(x) \cdot Q(x) + R(x)$.

11-1

1. $P(x) = x^3 + 3x^2 - x - 10$
    a. $D(x) = x - 2$ _____

    b. $D(x) = x + 1$ _____

2. $P(x) = x^3 + 8$
    a. $D(x) = x + 2$ _____

    b. $D(x) = x - 3$ _____

3. $P(x) = 3x^5 + 4x^3 - 2x^2 + 6$
    a. $D(x) = x - 1$ _____

    b. $D(x) = x^2 + 2$ _____

4. $P(x) = 8x^7 + 4x^6 - 3x^3 + 9x^2 + 8$
    a. $D(x) = x + 1$ _____

    b. $D(x) = 2x^2 + x - 1$ _____

Consider the following functions. Find the indicated function values.

3-3

5. $f(x) = \dfrac{x^2 + x - 2}{2x^2 + 3x - 9}$

    a. $f(2)$ _____   **b.** $f(-3)$ _____   **c.** $f(-2)$ _____

6. $g(x) = \dfrac{2x^2 + 7x + 3}{3x + 5}$

    a. $g\left(-\dfrac{5}{3}\right)$ _____   **b.** $g(-3)$ _____   **c.** $g(1)$ _____

Suppose $f(x) = x^2 + 1$, $g(x) = x - 2$, and $h(x) = 3x$. Find the following.

3-9

7. $f(g(2))$ _____

9. $h(f(-3))$ _____

8. $g(h(-4))$ _____

10. $g(f(x))$ _____

Find the function values

11-2

11. $P(x) = x^3 - 3x^2 - 6x + 8$
    $P(1)$ _____, $P(2)$ _____,
    $P(-3)$ _____

12. $P(x) = x^5 + x^4 - 5x^3 - 5x^2 - 36x - 36$
    $P(-2)$ _____, $P(3)$ _____,
    $P(2)$ _____

Divide.

16-1

13. $(a^3 + 2a - 12) \div (a + 3)$ _____

14. $(y^4 - y^2 - 30) \div (y^2 - 6)$ _____

16-4

15. $\dfrac{x^2 - 49}{x^2 + 9x + 14} \div \dfrac{3x - 21}{x^2 - x - 6}$ _____

Find a polynomial of lowest degree with rational coefficients that has the given numbers as some of its roots.

11-3

16. $1 - i, 2$ _____

18. $2i, \sqrt{2}$ _____

20. $-i, 2 + i\sqrt{2}$ _____

17. $1 + i, -2$ _____

19. $3i, -\sqrt{3}$ _____

21. $\sqrt{3}, -1 - i\sqrt{5}$ _____

Find an equation of a parabola with vertex at the origin satisfying the given conditions.

10-5

1. Focus $(3, 0)$ _____ **2.** Focus $(0, 2\pi)$ _____

Graph each polynomial. Find approximate roots to the nearest tenth.

11-6

3. $P(x) = x^4 - 5x^2 + 6$ _____ **4.** $P(x) = x^4 - 7x^2 + 12$ _____

5. $P(x) = x^4 - 3x^2 + 2$ _____ **6.** $P(x) = x^4 - 3x^2 + 1$ _____

Tell which conic is defined by each equation.

10-6

7. $3x^2 + 3y^2 - 4x + 5y + 1 = 0$ _____ **8.** $4x^2 - 5y^2 + 6x + 4 = 0$ _____

9. $-5x^2 - 7y^2 + 14x + y + 1 = 0$ _____ **10.** $-2x^2 - 2y^2 + 8x - 3y = 0$ _____

11. $9y^2 + 8x - 3y + 5 = 0$ _____ **12.** $13x^2 + 17y^2 - 14 = 0$ _____

Solve.

10-8

13. A new shopping mall will consist of two square
buildings separated by a small park. Find the length
of each building if the sum of their areas is 9700 m^2
and the difference of their areas is 6500 m^2. _____

Find the rational roots, if they exist, of each polynomial. Find the other roots, if possible.

11-4

14. $P(x) = x^3 + 3x^2 - 3x - 9$ _____ **15.** $P(x) = 3x^3 + x^2 + 12x + 4$ _____

16. $P(x) = x^4 + x^3 + x^2 + 3x - 6$ _____ **17.** $P(x) = x^3 + 27$ _____

18. $P(x) = 4x^3 - 9x^2 + 10x - 2$ _____ **19.** $P(x) = 2x^4 - 9x^3 + 3x^2 + 11x - 3$ _____

Use Descartes' rule of signs to determine the number of (a) positive real roots and
(b) negative real roots.

11-5

20. $P(x) = 2x^4 - 6x^3 - 5x^2 - 3x + 5$ **a.** _____ **b.** _____

21. $P(x) = -4x^2 - 3x - 9$ **a.** _____ **b.** _____

22. $P(x) = x^3 - x^2 + 3x - 4$ **a.** _____ **b.** _____

23. $P(x) = x^5 + 5x^4 - x^3 + 5x^2 - 5x + 1$ **a.** _____ **b.** _____

Use the sum and the product properties to write a quadratic equation whose solutions are
the following.

8-4

24. $2, 4$ _____ **25.** $-3, \dfrac{3}{4}$ _____

26. $3 + \sqrt{3}, 3 - \sqrt{3}$ _____ **27.** $3 + 3i, 3 - 3i$ _____

Find equations for $f^{-1}(x)$ for the following.

12-1
1. $f(x) = x - 8$ _____
2. $f(x) = x + 5$ _____
3. $f(x) = 5x - 3$ _____

4. $f(x) = 2x + 6$ _____
5. $f(x) = \sqrt{x + 1}$ _____
6. $f(x) = \sqrt{x - 3}$ _____

Graph. Where possible, use transformations.

12-2
7. $y = 4^x$
8. $y = (3.5)^x$
9. $y = \left(\dfrac{1}{3}\right)^x$
10. $y = (0.9)^x$

11. $y = \log_4 x$
12. $y = \log_{3.5} x$
13. $y = \log \dfrac{1}{3} x$
14. $y = \log_{0.9} x$

Solve.

2-1
15. $4x - 12 = 7x + 3$ _____
16. $7 - 2y = 5y - 13$ _____

17. $3(x + 4) = 4x$ _____
18. $(t - 3)(2t + 1) = 0$ _____

5-7
19. $6x^2 + 11x = 10$ _____
20. $81x^2 = 16$ _____

12-3
21. $\log_x 36 = 2$ _____
22. $\log_4 x = 3$ _____

23. $\log_3 x = 4$ _____
24. $\log_9 x = -2$ _____

Express in terms of logarithms of p, q, and r.

12-4
25. $\log_a p^3 q^2 r$ _____
26. $\log_a 3p^2 q^5$ _____

27. $\log_b \dfrac{pq^2}{r^4}$ _____
28. $\log_b \dfrac{p^3}{q^2 r^6}$ _____

Express as a single logarithm. Simplify, if possible.

12-4
29. $\log_a 5 + \log_a 30$ _____
30. $\log_a x + \log_a h$ _____

31. $\dfrac{1}{3} \log_b x - \dfrac{1}{2} \log_b y$ _____
32. $3 \log_b \sqrt[3]{x} - 2 \log_b x$ _____

33. $\log_c 4y + 2(\log_c y - \log_c x)$ _____
34. $\log_c \dfrac{b}{\sqrt{x}} - \dfrac{1}{2} \log_c x^2$ _____

Given $\log_{10} 3 \approx 0.477$, $\log_{10} 4 \approx 0.602$, and $\log_{10} 5 \approx 0.699$, find the following.

12-4
35. $\log_{10} 12$ _____
36. $\log_{10} 60$ _____
37. $\log_{10} 36$ _____

Find only the rational roots.

11-4
38. $P(x) = x^4 + 3x^3 - 4x^2 - 18x - 12$ _____

39. $P(x) = x^4 - 5x^3 - x^2 + 35x - 42$ _____

Use a calculator, Table 2, or Table 3 to find these logarithms.

12-5

1. log 3.42 _____ **2.** log 7.31 _____ **3.** log 9.56 _____

4. log 827 _____ **5.** log 40,600 _____ **6.** log 0.00598 _____

12-8

7. ln 3.67 _____ **8.** ln 2.45 _____ **9.** ln 24.5 _____

10. ln 0.00245 _____ **11.** ln 34,200 _____ **12.** ln 0.05 _____

Use a calculator or Table 2 to find these antilogarithms.

12-6

13. antilog 0.5353 _____ **14.** antilog 0.7388 _____

15. antilog 5.3032 _____ **16.** antilog (3.8774 − 10) _____

17. antilog (4.9330 − 10) _____ **18.** antilog (5.6599 − 10) _____

Solve.

7-6

19. $\sqrt{3x - 1} = 2$ _____ **20.** $\sqrt[3]{2x + 4} + 7 = 4$ _____

21. $2\sqrt{2y - 1} = \sqrt{7y + 1}$ _____ **22.** $\sqrt{4y + 9} - \sqrt{5y - 4} = 1$ _____

7-10

23. $(4 + i)x - i = 5$ _____ **24.** $(5 - i)x + 3 = 2 - 4i + 3ix$ _____

8-3

25. $6x^2 + 7x + 2 = 0$ _____ **26.** $t^2 + 7 = 0$ _____

27. $a^2 + 6a + 4 = 0$ _____ **28.** $-2(x + 2)^2 + (x - 1)^2 = 0$ _____

8-5

29. $b^4 - 6b^2 + 5 = 0$ _____ **30.** $6x^{-2} - 5x^{-1} - 6 = 0$ _____

31. $z^{\frac{2}{3}} - z^{\frac{1}{3}} - 6 = 0$ _____ **32.** $w^{\frac{1}{2}} + w^{\frac{1}{4}} - 2 = 0$ _____

12-7

33. $3^x = 27$ _____ **34.** $3^x = 40$ _____ **35.** $2^{3x-10} = 32$ _____

36. $4^{x^2 + 4x} = \frac{1}{64}$ _____ **37.** $3^{x+1} = 4^{x-1}$ _____ **38.** $(2.2)^x = 34$ _____

39. $\log x - \log (x - 9) = 1$ _____ **40.** $\log_3 (x + 3) + \log_3 (x - 3) = 4$ _____

41. $\log \sqrt[5]{x} = \sqrt{\log x}$ _____ **42.** $\log \sqrt[3]{x^4} + \log \sqrt[3]{x^5} = \log 2^{-4}$ _____

12-8

43. One of the most therapeutic uses of nuclear medicine is the use of iodine-131 in the treatment of thyroid cancer. Iodine is trapped in the thyroid at a level 25 times that of blood for the production of thyroid hormone. If the half-life of I-131 is 8 days, how much of a sample will remain after 24 days? After 60 days? _____

For the Exercises on this page, let

$$A = \begin{bmatrix} 2 & 3 \\ 5 & -4 \end{bmatrix} \quad B = \begin{bmatrix} -2 & -6 \\ 3 & -1 \end{bmatrix} \quad C = \begin{bmatrix} 1 & -1 \\ -1 & 1 \end{bmatrix} \quad D = \begin{bmatrix} 1 & 1 \\ 1 & 1 \end{bmatrix} \quad E = \begin{bmatrix} 7 & 1 \\ 8 & 5 \end{bmatrix}$$

$$F = \begin{bmatrix} -2 & 0 & 1 \\ -1 & 3 & 0 \\ 4 & -2 & 3 \end{bmatrix} \quad G = \begin{bmatrix} -1 & -2 & 6 \\ -1 & 0 & 1 \\ -6 & -5 & 1 \end{bmatrix} \quad H = \begin{bmatrix} 7 & -3 & 2 \\ -4 & 1 & 5 \end{bmatrix} \quad I = \begin{bmatrix} -5 & 6 \\ 4 & 3 \\ -2 & -8 \end{bmatrix}$$

Find the dimensions of each matrix.

13-1   **1.** C _____   **2.** G _____   **3.** H _____   **4.** I _____

Add.

13-2   **5.** $A + B$ _____   **6.** $C + E$ _____   **7.** $F + G$ _____

Subtract by adding an additive inverse.

13-2   **8.** $A - B$ _____   **9.** $E - C$ _____   **10.** $D - B$ _____

11. $B - A$ _____   **12.** $F - G$ _____   **13.** $G - F$ _____

Multiply.

13-4   **14.** $(-2)A$ _____   **15.** qE _____   **16.** $(-6)G$ _____

17. AB _____   **18.** DE _____   **19.** GF _____

Find each product, if possible.

13-4   **20.** HI _____   **21.** IH _____   **22.** IF _____

23. BH _____   **24.** ID _____   **25.** HF _____

Solve each formula for the given letter.

8-6   **26.** $a^2 + b^2 = c^2; c$ _____   **27.** $t = \sqrt{\dfrac{2s}{g}}; s$ _____

28. $V = \pi r^2 h; r$ _____   **29.** $x = 2vt + 10t^2; t$ _____

Evaluate.

13-3

1. $\begin{vmatrix} 2 & 3 \\ 4 & 5 \end{vmatrix}$ _____

2. $\begin{vmatrix} 1 & -4 \\ 2 & -7 \end{vmatrix}$ _____

3. $\begin{vmatrix} 3 & 6 \\ -1 & -4 \end{vmatrix}$ _____

4. $\begin{vmatrix} 1 & 0 & 2 \\ -1 & 2 & 0 \\ 2 & 1 & 1 \end{vmatrix}$ _____

5. $\begin{vmatrix} -2 & 2 & 1 \\ -1 & 2 & 4 \\ 4 & -2 & 1 \end{vmatrix}$ _____

6. $\begin{vmatrix} 3 & 4 & 5 \\ 2 & 1 & 6 \\ 9 & 8 & 7 \end{vmatrix}$ _____

Simplify.

6-3

7. $\dfrac{\frac{1}{a} + 3}{\frac{1}{a} - 2}$ _____

8. $\dfrac{y - \frac{1}{y}}{y + \frac{1}{y}}$ _____

9. $\dfrac{\frac{4}{x} + \frac{5}{y}}{\frac{5}{x} - \frac{4}{y}}$ _____

10. $\dfrac{\frac{a^2 - b^2}{ab}}{\frac{a - b}{a}}$ _____

Find A^{-1}, if it exists.

13-5

11. $A = \begin{bmatrix} 2 & 3 \\ 4 & 5 \end{bmatrix}$ _____

13. $A = \begin{bmatrix} 1 & -4 \\ 2 & -7 \end{bmatrix}$ _____

13. $A = \begin{bmatrix} 3 & 6 \\ 2 & 5 \end{bmatrix}$ _____

14. $\begin{bmatrix} \frac{1}{2} & 4 \\ 1 & 8 \end{bmatrix}$ _____

13-6

15. $A = \begin{bmatrix} -2 & 2 & 1 \\ -1 & 2 & 4 \\ 4 & -2 & 1 \end{bmatrix}$ _____

16. $A = \begin{bmatrix} -3 & 1 & 1 \\ -1 & 3 & 0 \\ 1 & -2 & 0 \end{bmatrix}$ _____

Solve graphically.

4-1

17. $2x + 3y = 4$
$4x + 5y = 6$ _____

18. $x - 4y = -3$
$2x + 7y = 24$ _____

19. $2x + 7y = 5$
$8x + 9y = 1$ _____

13-3

Solve the systems in Exercises 18–20 using Cramer's rule.

20. _____

21. _____

22. _____

11-2

23. Let $P(x) = x^3 - 4x^2 + x + 6$

a. Find a complete factorization of $P(x)$. _____

b. Solve the equation $P(x) = 0$. _____

MIXED REVIEW 27

For use after Lesson 14-2

NAME _____

DATE _____

The general term of a sequence is given. In each case find the first four terms and the 12th term.

14-1

1. $a_n = 3n + 3$ _____ **2.** $a_n = 3n - 3$ _____

3. $a_n = n^2 + 3n$ _____ **4.** $a_n = n^2 - 2$ _____

5. $a_n = \left(-\dfrac{1}{3}\right)^{n+1}$ _____ **6.** $a_n = \dfrac{n^2}{n^2 + 1}$ _____

Find S_1, S_2, S_3, and S_4 for each sequence in Exercises 1-6.

14-1

7. _____ **8.** _____ **9.** _____

10. _____ **11.** _____ **12.** _____

Write a matrix equation equivalent to each of the following systems of equations.

13-4

13. $2x - 3y + z = 4$
$x + y - z = -1$
$-5x + y + 4z = 5$ _____

14. $-x + 2y - 4z = -1$
$2x + 5y + z = 6$
$x - 7z = 4$ _____

15. $3x - 5y = 8$
$y + 6z = -7$
$x + z = 3$ _____

16. $2y + z = 0$
$-4x + 3z = 6$
$7x - 5y = -3$ _____

For the arithmetic sequences in Exercises 17 and 18, find the 18th term and the common difference.

14-2

17. $3, 1, -1, -3, \ldots$ _____ **18.** $0.11, 0.16, 0.21, 0.26, \ldots$ _____

19. In the sequence $2, \dfrac{7}{2}, 5, \ldots$, what term has a value of $\dfrac{37}{2}$? _____

20. The 14th term of an arithmetic sequence is 1 and the 25th term is 100. Find a_1 and d. Construct the sequence. _____

Test for symmetry with respect to the x-axis, the y-axis, the origin, and the line $y = x$.

12-1

21. $2x = y^2 + 3$ _____ **22.** $4y - 3x^2 = 5$ _____

23. $6x^4 + 2y^2 = 7$ _____ **24.** $2xy^3 = 7$ _____

25. $2x^3 + 2y^3 = 9$ _____ **26.** $3y^2 = 7 - 4x^2$ _____

27. $3x = 4 - 3y$ _____ **28.** $xy = 4$ _____

Find the common ratio and the 8th term for each geometric sequence.

14-3   **1.** $2, 6, 18, 54, \ldots$ _____   **2.** $3, 6p, 12p^2, 24p^3, \ldots$ _____

Find the sum of the first 8 terms of the following geometric series.

14-3   **3.** $3 + 6 + 12 + \cdots$ _____   **4.** $200 - 50 + 12.5 - \cdots$ _____

Find the sum of each geometric series.

14-3   **5.** $\displaystyle\sum_{k=1}^{10} 3^k$ _____   **6.** $\displaystyle\sum_{k=1}^{8} \left(\frac{1}{4}\right)^k$ _____   **7.** $\displaystyle\sum_{k=1}^{7} (0.5)^{k+1}$ _____

Multiply and simplify.

6-1   **8.** $\dfrac{x^2 + 6x + 9}{x^2 + x - 6} \cdot \dfrac{x^2 - 4}{x^2 + 5x + 6}$ _____   **9.** $\dfrac{2x - y}{5x^2 + 3xy - 2y^2} \cdot \dfrac{x^2 - y^2}{2x^2 - 3xy + y^2}$ _____

Use the principle of mathematical induction to prove each of the following.

14-5   **10.** $1 + 2 + 3 + \cdots + n = \dfrac{n(n+1)}{2}$ _____   **11.** $\dfrac{1}{2} + \dfrac{1}{2^2} + \dfrac{1}{2^3} + \cdots + \dfrac{1}{2^n} = 1 - \dfrac{1}{2^n}$ _____

Find a polynomial of degree 3 with the given numbers as roots.

11-3   **12.** $4, 2, 1$ _____   **13.** $3i, -3i, 3$ _____

       14. $2 + 2i, 2 - 2i, 2$ _____   **15.** $\sqrt{5}, -\sqrt{5}, \sqrt{3}$ _____

Solve.

11-3   **16.** Find a polynomial of degree 5 with -3 as a root of multiplicity 3 and 2 as a root of multiplicity 2. _____

14-2   **17.** Insert four arithmetic means between 4 and 24. _____

       18. Insert five arithmetic means between -4 and 5. _____

14-3   **19.** Insert two geometric means between 1 and 8. _____

       20. Insert three geometric means between 4 and $\dfrac{1}{4}$. _____

Find the sum of each series.

14-2   **21.** $\displaystyle\sum_{n=1}^{13} (2n + 15)$ _____   **22.** $\displaystyle\sum_{n=1}^{20} 7k$ _____   **23.** $\displaystyle\sum_{n=1}^{14} (4n - 12)$ _____

Solve.

15-1   **1.** In how many ways can 6 football players position themselves on the line of scrimmage?

_____

15-1   **2.** How many ordered codes can be formed of the set $\{S, F, U, N, I, O\}$

      a. using 6 letters allowing repetition? _____

      b. using 5 letters allowing repetition? _____

      c. using 4 letters allowing repetition? _____

      d. using 5 letters without repetition? _____

      e. using 5 letters that are not repeated but must end with N? _____

15-1   **3.** How many permutations are there with the letters in the set $\{S, F, U, N, I, O\}$? _____

Evaluate.

15-1   **4.** $_6P_6$ _____   **5.** $_4P_4$ _____   **6.** $_1P_1$ _____

15-1   **7.** $_8P_2$ _____   **8.** $_7P_4$ _____   **9.** $_{20}P_5$ _____

15-3   **10.** $\binom{20}{5}$ _____   **11.** $\binom{52}{4}$ _____   **12.** $\binom{11}{4}$ _____

15-2   **13.** In how many ways can 11 football players arrange themselves in a huddle? _____

Write sigma notation for each sum.

14-1   **14.** $6 + 9 + 12 + 15 + 18$ _____   **15.** $1^2 + 3^2 + 5^2 + 7^2$ _____

      16. $2 - 4 + 8 - 16 + 32$ _____   **17.** $-1 + 2 + 7 + 14 + 23 + 34$ _____

9-7   **18.** Determine the equation of the function from its graph.

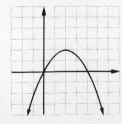

MIXED REVIEW 30
For use after Lesson 15-7

NAME _____

DATE _____

Suppose we draw a card from a deck of 52 cards. What is the probability of drawing

15-5 **1.** a face card? _____ **2.** a spade? _____ **3.** a 4 or a 5? _____

15-6 **4.** a club or a king? _____ **5.** a red card or a face card? _____

15-5 **6.** What is the probability of getting a total of 9 on a roll of a pair of dice? _____

7. From a group of 6 men and 9 women, a committee of 4 is chosen. What is the probability that 2 men and 2 women will be chosen? _____

A die is rolled twice. What is the probability of rolling

15-6 **8.** a 4 on the first roll and a 4 on the second roll? _____

9. an even number on the first row and an odd number on the second roll? _____

10. a multiple of two on the first roll and a multiple of three on the second roll? _____

3-8 **11.** If a linear function fits the data, determine the function, and predict mi/g for an average speed of 65 mi/h, and predict the average speed that will deliver 20 mi/g.

Average speed (mi/h)	35	40	45	50	55
Miles per gal.	38	37	34	32	28

_____

_____

_____

12. If a linear function fits the data, determine the function, predict the number of cells after 8 minutes, and predict how long it will take to have 100 cells.

Time (min)	1	2	3	4	5
Cells	1	2	4	7	15

_____

_____

_____

8-8 **13.** Fit a quadratic function through $(-1, 4)$, $(2, -2)$, and $(0, 7)$. _____

Simplify.

12-3 **14.** $5^{\log_5 13}$ _____ **15.** $\log_r r^7$ _____ **16.** $\log_z z^r$ _____

Express as a sum or a difference of logarithms.

12-4 **17.** $\log_a \dfrac{13}{5}$ _____ **18.** $\log_a xy$ _____ **19.** $\log_b \dfrac{cd}{z}$ _____

4-3 **1.** The Rookie of the Year award in the Southern Baseball League is based upon points given for first place, second place, and third-place votes. Nel Stone received 85 points from 9 first-place votes, 5 second-place votes, and 2 third-place votes. Jo Santiago had 65 points from 4 firsts, 11 seconds, and 3 thirds. Oddibe Johnson had 39 points from 1 first, 5 seconds, and 12 thirds. How many points is a vote for each place worth?

_____

16-1 Use the following data for Problems 2–5.

The ages of 10 recent presidents at their first inaugurations were as follows:

  51, 60, 62, 43, 55, 56, 61, 52, 69, 64

2. Construct a stem-and-leaf diagram.

Stem	Leaf

16-2 **3.** What is the mean age?

_____

4. What is the median age?

_____

5. Is there a mode age? If so, what is it?

_____

10-6 **6.** Determine the equation of the conic from its graph.

_____

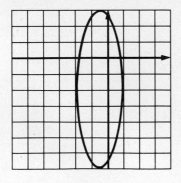

15-5   **1.** A die is thrown twice. What is the probability that neither throw will result in a number greater than 2? _____

    2. Six cards are marked 1, 2, 3, 4, 5, and 6. Two cards are chosen from the six cards. What is the probability that neither card is marked with a number greater than 2? _____

4-6   **3.** Determine whether the system is dependent. _____
$$3x - 4y = 1$$
$$8x - 6y = 2$$

3-9 $f(x) = 2x - 3$ and $g(x) = x^2 - 4$.

    4. Find an expression for $f(g(x))$. _____

    5. Find an expression for $g(f(x))$. _____

    6. Find an expression for $f(f(x))$. _____

    7. Find an expression for $g(g(x))$. _____

16-3   Use the following data for Problems 8–10.
        1, 13, 5, 9, 3, 11, 7

    8. What is the mean deviation? _____

    9. What is the variance? _____

    10. What is the standard deviation? _____

14-2   **11.** Find the arithmetic mean between 9 and 36. _____

14-3   **12.** Find the geometric mean between 9 and 36. _____

6-9   **13.** If $y = 36$ when $x = 9$, and y varies directly with x, find the equation of direct variation. _____

    14. If $y = 36$ when $x = 9$, and y varies inversely with x, find the equation of inverse variation. _____

8-7   **15.** If $y = 36$ when $x = 9$, and y varies directly with the square of x, find the equation of variation. _____

Find sin θ, cos θ, tan θ, csc θ, sec θ, cot θ. Use rational notation.

17-1   **1.**

2.

_____   _____

17-3   **3.**

4.

_____   _____

Give the sign of the six trigonometric function values and the reference angle for the following angles of rotation.

17-2   **5.** $78°$ _____   **6.** $222°$ _____

7. $500°$ _____   **8.** $-14°$ _____

9. $-100°$ _____   **10.** $100°$ _____

Use Table 5 to find the following.

17-4   **11.** sin $17°40'$ _____   **12.** sec $41°10'$ _____   **13.** cot $177°50'$ _____

14. tan $310°20'$ _____   **15.** cos $220°40'$ _____   **16.** csc $500°30'$ _____

Convert to exponential equations.

12-3   **17.** $3 = \log_5 125$ _____   **18.** $a = \log_5 7$ _____

19. $8 = \log_b 13$ _____   **20.** $11 = \log_2 c$ _____

Convert to degrees and minutes.

17-4   **21.** $53.14°$ _____   **22.** $-20.35°$ _____   **23.** $516.78°$ _____

Convert to degrees and decimal parts of degrees.

17-4   **24.** $8°14'$ _____   **25.** $-187°36'$ _____   **26.** $392°51'$ _____

Find identities for the following.

17-6   **1.** $\tan\left(\dfrac{\pi}{2} - \theta\right)$ _____   **2.** $\cot\left(\dfrac{\pi}{2} - \theta\right)$ _____

3. $\sec\left(\theta - \dfrac{\pi}{2}\right)$ _____   **4.** $\csc\left(\theta - \dfrac{\pi}{2}\right)$ _____

Sketch graphs of these functions. Determine the amplitude and the period.

17-7   **5.** $y = 2\sin\theta$ _____   **6.** $y = \cos 2\theta$ _____

7. $y = \cos\left(-\dfrac{1}{4}\theta\right)$ _____   **8.** $y = 3\sin 3\theta$ _____

9. $y = 2\cos\left(-\dfrac{1}{2}\theta\right)$ _____   **10.** $y = \dfrac{1}{3}\sin 2\theta$ _____

Multiply and simplify.

7-9   **11.** $\sqrt{-5} \cdot 5i$ _____   **12.** $(2 - 5i)^2$ _____

7-2   **13.** $\sqrt[3]{2x^2}\,\sqrt[3]{2x^2}$ _____   **14.** $\sqrt[3]{3x^2y^4}\,\sqrt[3]{x^4y^4}$ _____

5-3   **15.** $(3a^2 - b)^3$ _____   **16.** $(u + 3v)(3u - v)$ _____

17-8   **17.** $\tan x(\cos x - \csc x)$ _____   **18.** $(1 + \cot x)^2$ _____

19. $\cos x \sin x(\csc x + \sec x)$ _____   **20.** $(\sin x - \csc x)^2$ _____

Factor the polynomial $P(x)$.

11-2   **21.** $P(x) = x^3 - 13x + 12$ _____   **22.** $P(x) = x^3 + 6x^2 + 5x - 12$ _____

23. $P(x) = x^3 - 3x^2 - 4x + 12$ _____   **24.** $P(x) = x^3 - 5x^2 - 2x + 24$ _____

Factor and simplify.

17-8   **25.** $\sin^4 x - \cos^4 x$ _____   **26.** $\sin^2 x - \sin^2 x \cos^2 x$ _____

27. $4\sec^2 x + 8\sec x + 4$ _____   **28.** $\dfrac{\tan x \cos^2 x + \tan x \sin^2 x}{\sin x}$ _____

Simplify.

17-8   **29.** $\dfrac{\sec^2 x \csc x}{\csc^2 x \sec x}$ _____   **30.** $\dfrac{\cos^2 \theta \sin \theta}{\sin^2 \theta \cos \theta}$ _____

31. $(2 + \sqrt{\sin \theta})(2 - \sqrt{\sin \theta})$ _____

Use sum and difference identities to simplify the following.

18-1

1. $\cos(45° - 60°)$ _____

2. $\sin(45° - 60°)$ _____

3. $\cos\left(\dfrac{\pi}{3} - \dfrac{\pi}{4}\right)$ _____

4. $\sin\left(\dfrac{\pi}{3} - \dfrac{\pi}{4}\right)$ _____

Use sum and difference formulas to find the following.

18-1

5. $\sin 75°$ _____

6. $\cos 150°$ _____

7. $\tan 195°$ _____

Find $\sin 2\theta$, $\cos 2\theta$, $\tan 2\theta$, and the quadrant in which 2θ lies.

18-2

8. $\sin\theta = -\dfrac{4}{5}$ (θ in quadrant III) _____

9. $\tan\theta = -\dfrac{12}{5}$ (θ in quadrant II) _____

Prove these identities.

18-3

10. $\csc\theta \tan\theta = \sec\theta$

11. $\sin 2\theta = \dfrac{2\tan\theta}{1 + \tan^2\theta}$

12. $\dfrac{\cos x}{\cot x} = \dfrac{\tan x}{\sec x}$

Find all values of the following.

18-4

13. $\arccos\left(-\dfrac{1}{2}\right)$ _____

14. $\csc^{-1}\dfrac{2\sqrt{3}}{3}$ _____

15. $\operatorname{arccot} 1$ _____

16. $\sec^{-1}(-1)$ _____

18-4

Find the following without using a table or a calculator.

17. $\operatorname{Tan}^{-1} 0$ _____

18. $\operatorname{Cos}^{-1} 0$ _____

19. $\operatorname{Sin}^{-1}(-1)$ _____

18-5

Solve. Find all solutions from 0 to 2π.

20. $2\sin^2 x = 1$ _____

21. $2\cos^2 x = -3\cos x - 1$ _____

22. $\cos x = \sin 2x$ _____

17-1

Find the length of each labeled side.

23.

24.

25.

_____

_____

_____

Convert to logarithmic equations.

12-3   **1.** $y^4 = 5$ _____   **2.** $3^5 = z$ _____

Given that the polynomial has the given root, find all roots of the polynomial.

11-3   **3.** $P(x) = x^4 - 4x^3 + 3x^2 + 20x - 40;$ $2 + 2i$ _____

4. $P(x) = x^4 - 6x^3 + 3x^2 + 42x - 70;$ $-\sqrt{7}$ _____

Solve the triangles using three-digit precision. In each case, angle C is a right angle.

18-6   **5.** $m\angle A = 14°, a = 6$ _____

6. $m\angle A = 65°, b = 5$ _____

7. $b = 15, c = 45$ _____

Solve triangle ABC.

18-7   **8.** $a = 25, b = 10, m\angle A = 42°$ _____

9. $m\angle C = 118°, a = 6, b = 10$ _____

10. $a = 4.1, b = 2.2, c = 2.4$ _____

Convert to trigonometric notation and then multiply or divide.

18-9   **11.** $(-5\sqrt{3} + 5i)(-2 - 2i\sqrt{3})$ _____   **12.** $(\sqrt{2} + i\sqrt{2})(-3 + 3i\sqrt{3})$ _____

13. $\dfrac{-6\sqrt{3} + 6i}{-2 - 2i\sqrt{3}}$ _____   **14.** $\dfrac{-7 + 7i\sqrt{3}}{\sqrt{2} + i\sqrt{2}}$ _____

Raise the number to the power. Give your answer in rectangular notation.

18-9   **15.** $(4 \text{ cis } 150°)^3$ _____   **16.** $(4 \text{ cis } 225°)^3$ _____

17. $\left(\dfrac{\sqrt{3}}{2} - \dfrac{1}{2}i\right)^{14}$ _____   **18.** $(\sqrt{2} - i\sqrt{2})^{10}$ _____

Factor the polynomial $P(x)$. Then solve the equation $P(x) = 0$.

11-2   **19.** $P(x) = x^3 + 6x^2 + 11x + 6$ _____

20. $P(x) = x^3 + 4x^2 + x - 6$ _____

21. $P(x) = x^4 + x^3 - 19x^2 + 11x + 30$ _____

22. $P(x) = x^4 - 4x^3 - 7x^2 + 22x + 24$ _____